# THE COMPLETE GUIDE TO
# GATECRASHING

# THE COMPLETE GUIDE TO
# GATECRASHING

## Nicholas Allan

EBURY
PRESS

**To Jaqui and Victor – my learned friends**

First published in Great Brtain in 2001
This edition published in 2001
1 3 5 7 9 10 8 6 4 2
text and illustrations ©2001 Nicholas Allan

Every effort has been made to trace the copyright owners of the Bateman
cartoon that appears on page 17 of this book.

Ebury Press
Random House, 20 Vauxhall Bridge Road, London SW1V 2SA
Random House Australia Pty
20 Alfred Street, Milsons Point, Sydney, New South Wales 2061, Australia
Random House New Zealand Limited
18 Poland Road, Glenfield, Auckland 10, New Zealand
Random House, South Africa (Pty) Limited
Endulini, 5A Jubilee Road, Parktown 2193, South Africa
Random House Group Limited Reg.No. 954009

www.randomhouse.co.uk
A CIP catalogue record for this book is available from the British Library

ISBN 0091881188

Cover design by The Senate
Design by Sue Casebourne
Editorial by Cover (to) Cover a.t.e.
Printed and bound in Denmark by Nørhaven AS.

Papers used by Ebury Press are natural, recyclable products made from
wood grown in sustainable forests.

# CONTENTS

# INTRODUCTION

## The Best Things In Life – Taittinger, Beluga Caviar, Château-Neuf du Pape – Are Free

Just as there is nothing new under the sun, there is no such thing as a free lunch. Really? I have often wondered if this last cliché was deliberately concocted by the creatively minded to inhibit experimentation by others. That there are new things under the sun is patently obvious. (People shown the first microwave oven must've thought it was a conjuring trick: the fish cooked, the oven and plate cold.) I quickly discovered the business about free lunches is equally fallacious and misinformed – even if I realise now why people in the know might like to keep quiet about it.

I was reluctant, at first, to divulge the secrets of successful gatecrashing. For the last three years, my evenings (rather than my money) have been spent drinking excellent champagne, attending Savoy dinners, in good company – from Mick Jagger to Harold Pinter – and enjoying the best seats at plays and concerts for nothing.

The *Big Issue* ran an article on salad-bar plate stacking. It explained how to double the plate area by laying down a foundation of lettuce leaves extending over the plate lip, cementing the leaves in place with pâté or coleslaw, then building the salad on top. Soon after, the restaurants with help-yourself salad bars had their lettuce chopped into very tiny pieces.

In bars I only pay supermarket prices, and I have a cupboard full of expensive gifts donated by generous party hosts.

The interest people have shown when I've mentioned my hobby, coupled with the irresistible compulsion for hobby enthusiasts – from racing-snail breeders to collectors of Russian icons – to bore anyone who'll listen, compels me to tell.

I was given added incentive when a *Big Issue* seller told me a better, much more efficient method of plate stacking (*see page 9*) had recently been evolved.

There is one other reason too – a reason that goes a little deeper than you might expect from the subject matter – but this reason will only become clear as you read the book.

**A Note** *As I live in London, many of the venues mentioned are in the city, but of course, like football and chess, gatecrashing is a universal sport: the rules are the same. In fact, I've crashed some of my best dinners and parties in foreign hotels and English towns. I once crashed a party in Swanage.*

# My First Time

I'll never forget it.

I was at the Royal Festival Hall to attend a tedious concert – Brahm's Requiem, probably – in which a friend was participating. Arriving early, I noticed people entering the inappropriately named 'People's Palace Restaurant' (it is expensive), which had been cleared of tables for a party. Trays of champagne were floating; a flunky stood with one by the door.

'Are you with the party, suh?' The tray swooped.

'Yes, but I'm waiting for a friend.'

'Would you care for a glass while you're waiting, suh?'

Taking a glass, I held it disbelievingly, took my first sip – and never looked back. The glass was a party invitation card. Soon I was standing by the windowed wall, waiting patiently for the hot buffet supper, looking out on a moonlit Thames, and beyond, over a Never-Never Land of winking lights below a turquoise sky, each light beckoning, each light a promise of another party like this. It was an epiphany, the discovery of a case of buried banknotes. This is how the Brink's-Mat Bank Robbers felt driving home. I'd accidentally dropped into Aladdin's cave: the world, I suddenly realised, was my party. If gatecrashing is an addiction, like smoking or shoplifting – which is exactly how it turned out to be for me – I was hooked.

# Why I Do It

I live alone in a flat with a view of Big Ben. Below, in the evening, the metropolis lights up. As a full-time writer, I can go for five days without talking to anyone. Saul Bellow said the great problem of a writer is what to do in the afternoon: mine is what to do in the evening. In addition, I live by my own rules, and one of them is never to drink alone.

Part of the reason for seeking nightly company is so I can have a drink. A writer wants company, but on their own terms. A party, especially a party of strangers, is the ideal milieu. The writer can talk and drink, then, as with other people's children, walk away.

## Dangermen

Unless you have a fatwa put on you, or are Ernest Hemingway, Aleksandr Solzhenitsyn or the Marquis de Sade, writing is a relatively safe activity. Like most readers, writers are intrigued by crime. Many would like the risk, danger and rewards, but not, of course, the prison sentence. Party crashing offers all but the last of these things: crashing bobs just below the thin line of illegality. Very few hosts would prosecute for a canapé.

## Everything is Free...

All these factors are expressed succinctly in the Bateman cartoon opposite. When I first saw this cartoon it brought to light a particular facet of my personality, and possibly Bateman's: the irresistible, perhaps universal, desire for a freebee.

The man who filled his fountain pen with the hotel ink

# The Uniform

Looking at early photos of the Kray twins, it doesn't surprise me that they spent the best part of their lives behind bars. They look as though they were born there – babies with scars, arm tattoos saying 'I luv mum' and double-breasted bibs. A master criminal should look like your Auntie May, your vicar or the old lady who does flower water colours at the adult art class, someone with hazel eyes, mild demeanor and a soft-toned voice.

● ● ● ● ● ● ● ● ● ● ● ● ● ● ● ● ●

## DRESS FOR SUCCESS

*It is always advantageous to dress well, even if you're just visiting the corner shop for a Mars Bar. At a routine appointment at my local hospital, I noticed a champagne reception and buffet about to begin in the main atrium. I hurried to my appointment, then joined the party after as a visiting consultant.*

● ● ● ● ● ● ● ● ● ● ● ● ● ● ● ● ●

The gatecrasher shouldn't look like a gatecrasher. Of course, there isn't, technically, a gatecrasher look. The expectation, though, would be someone badly groomed, furtive and sweaty, or pushy and brash, and liable to rapid inebriation. (I saw one once. I was passing through the gate at Buckingham Palace; behind me a man wearing an anorak, trainers and a Ken Dodd hairstyle was trying to gain entry using his weekly bus pass. Although demonstrating the lamentable standards of British gatecrashers, the amateur does provides a great decoy for the specialist.) For successful gatecrashing, the opposite should be the case. The secrets of success are immaculate clothes, immaculate manners and a gentle, even thoughtful, personality.

However, to actually gain entry to the party you must rely on an instantly favourable impression, so dress is of the first importance.

## Let's Party

When Big Ben sounds the cocktail hour, the PC is closed down, the party-list memorized and my elaborate preparations begin.

Even if a party guest spends the entire evening with a gatecrasher, the guest should, ideally, remember little about him or her. The gatecrasher deliberately adopts the blandness of a tax inspector or the official who checks your passport. You are, ideally, a ghost: you walk through walls. Although your clothes should be chosen to enhance this, it doesn't mean they shouldn't be very seriously expensive. By blandness, I mean classical and undemonstrative. If the clothes are expensive enough, they can be as effective as armour:

suspicion ricochets off you. (I was once sitting at a table at a champagne party in the Hilton when alerted officials – like ticket-inspectors – began circulating and checking invitation cards. Everyone at my table produced theirs. When it came to me. the inspector just nodded, and moved on.)

Preparations for crashing are much the same as preparing for a legitimate party, but there are crucial differences in terms of dress. In your wardrobe, the gatecrashing uniform should be kept separate from genuine party clothes, just as your work suits are segregated from your gym kit.

## Hot Pants

Standing in front of the bedroom mirror, the first thing you put on is your thermal underwear. The conscientious gatecrasher never wears a coat. Like a private detective, you might often be loitering discreetly at a street corner for up to half an hour, no joke when you consider the party season climaxes around the birth of Christ. (An interesting theological speculation is whether Jesus' date of birth was determined by his Father as a deliberate means to thwart future gatecrashers.) A pair of gloves, a scarf, a micro-umbrella and a foldable hat might be permissible. (*See THE MAGIC DOOR page 78 to discover the reason for these restrictions.*)

Otherwise, you are dependent on your thermals.

## HOT TIP

*An alternative is to deposit coats, bags etc. in the cloakroom of a nearby hotel. A busy restaurant with separate bar is a viable alternative. You deposit your coat, saying you'll be eating at the restaurant, but are meeting friends at the bar first. Then, when staff aren't looking, leave the premises. Before you go, check what time the restaurant closes.*

# The Suit

## The Men in Black

Men must, by necessity (*see ELASTICATED BLACK BOW TIE, opposite*), always wear a black suit, white shirt and a single-coloured tie (but not gold or silver, or Coco-the-Clown fluorescent pink.) Even for pop-star parties the elegant black suit is the badge of someone more important than the celebrities – the one, people suspect, who controls the money. The suit will be your most expensive item. The long cut of an Armani, for instance, is one to opt for; added elegance without people quite knowing why.

## Women and the LBD

As the primary requirement is anonymity, women are not much better off than men in choice. Stick with the Little Black Dress. A simple Dior frock, black too, or a sombre colour, is best. Women can afford, if that's the right word, several different LBDs; in fact, it's preferable, as it will help to deflect recognition after repeated crashes.

## ELASTICATED BLACK BOW TIE

I was attending a barely adequate reception at the Café Royale. I noticed a dinner-suited man climbing the stairs, so followed discreetly. In a ballroom a pre-drink reception was taking place for a corporate lawyers' annual dinner. Within minutes I found myself in the washroom, removing my chartreuse silk tie, and adjusting, like several other guests were doing with theirs, my black bow tie. I was beginning to feel hungry and wondered what was for dinner. I've enjoyed many Savoy dinners simply by following a couple of dinner jackets down the Strand.

Elastic is essential.

To paraphrase Spike Milligan:

*Cotton is thicker
But elastic is quicker.*

# Gadgets and Accessories

**Q-Branch**

After you've dressed, you must pocket your accessories – already lined up with military precision on your dressing table. Your party contact call might not come through until the last minute, so you must be as prepared for immediate flight as an on-duty fireman. Fastidious neatness of dress and equipment in the army is not just a neurotic quirk; it's to ensure that everything works and that nothing is forgotten.

## The Watch

It should be a wristwatch – no eccentric half-hunters on gold chains. A vital piece of equipment which should be completely reliable (timing is often crucial) and as visibly expensive as possible, the sort of watch you might expect Michael Winner to wear. It's difficult to think of a better description of a Rolex. (In fact, when I crashed a party of Mr Winner's, I noticed he didn't sport a watch. He did, however, smoke a very fat cigar.) As regards expense, like your clothes, to be seen as rich is to be seen as important, precluding all possible reason for a need to gatecrash. The general rule is: it's better to be thought of as vulgar and rich, than to be tasteful and run the risk of being thought poor.

### Notepad and Reliable Pen

Most people who go to parties usually have a motive other than pure, unadulterated oblivion. (One of these is often, of course, adultery itself.) The gatecrasher's motive is to acquire, by any means short of physical abuse, future party dates.

You never know when you might hit on a bonanza seam, beyond the trustworthiness of memory. The notebook should be as instantly available as a minder's automatic weapon.

My notebook is small, in a silver-plated case with a spring-release. It was, in fact, a parting gift from a corporate business annual party I crashed. It goes well with the Rolex.

## Business Cards

As your social life dilates, you'll find yourself with an abundant collection of business cards. In fact, it is one of the gatecrasher's duties to build up this collection. Like the collection of a fastidious

## TICKET TO RIDE

When travelling once in the first-class carriage of a train, without a first-class ticket or money, one of my cards proved very useful when the conductor asked to verify my name and address. Since then, in the dark silence of 2.30 a.m., I ponder in bed over what happened, if anything, to a certain impossibly rich city broker in Chancery Lane – a man, incidentally, who was actually proud of his Rolex Submariner.

philatelist, the cards should be sorted (according to profession) and carefully preserved. Aces are from journalists, the BBC, film companies. Don't, though, underestimate city lawyers, doctors and bankers. My own Royal Flush includes those of a Lloyds Bank Director and the Vice President of Universal Studios. I'm also, occasionally, a history professor of University College, London, and have been cardiac consultant at King's College Hospital.

## K-Rations

One last careful inspection in the bedroom mirror, then quickly return to the kitchen. In the fridge is already prepared a selection of portable food. This should include a boiled egg, small cuts of chicken breast wrapped in cling-film, individual mini-cheeses – all compact, high-protein foods you can eat on the hoof (or discreetly in a lavatory). Most guests arrive at parties with the expectation of food. This is greatly to your advantage, since they'll drink copiously first, the alcohol waltzing straight through the bloodstream as jubilantly as a virus.

Twenty minutes before the crash you crack open the egg, or unwrap the chicken, and line your stomach with protein. This has a dual effect. The first is that you remain relatively sober to begin with, while everyone else will already be having difficulties with their tongue articulation. The other important fact is that your stomach won't be screaming. It's essential not to be seen, like 'Smoked Salmon' Rushdie, or planet-girthed Patrick Moore, chasing after the canapé waiter all evening. Greed is noticed, and highly suspect.

## MINI HIGH-PRECISION TELESCOPE
### (Optional Extra)

*Those shops in Mayfair that sell bugging devices in a cigarette or a peanut, spy cameras and ankle knife holsters (shops presumably for secret agents who have forgotten to bring their own spy kit), are where you will find the mini-telescope. Before you enter the building where the party is held, you wait on the opposite side of the street, finishing your egg. It's to your advantage to know what's on the other side of the door. It might be two inebriated publicity girls; it could be ten guards gripping guest-lists and small firearms. As the guests arrive, the briefly opened door might provide what could be crucial information, the equivalent of a key or password. If the naked eye tells you a little, a telescope will enable you to read the small print.* (To know what it is you're supposed to be looking for, see THE MAGIC DOOR, page 78.)

Before that, though, you'll need to know where to
find the party...

# THE INFORMATION

One evening, peeing in the loo of Sanderson's Hotel, I heard an animated monologue issuing from one of the cubicles. The speaker, presumably (hopefully), was on a mobile, revealing details of a party – where his listener and he should meet.

As he flushed the loo, I quickly left and sat in the lounge eating my egg, waiting for the appointed time. The informer, his friend and I all arrived and entered the venue simultaneously, the official assuming I was with them.

# Where The Art Is

Information can be found, like germs, almost anywhere, and picked up as easily. For the beginner, the nursery slope of gatecrashing is the art gallery preview. It's more important for a gallery owner to discern a genuine Dior dress or Cartier watch than a genuine Raphael drawing or Warhol litho. If the gallery owners sees a stranger in an Armani enter the shop, he or she is more likely to phone for champagne than the police.

All gallery owners have Superman vision: he or she can see your invitation card, small, rectangular, and plastic, wedged in your wallet.

The gallery preview has one great advantage for the neophyte: it is the only kind of party you don't need to be seen in conversation. You can, in fact, be seen doing something very rare, which will particularly impress the owner, even the painter: you could look at the pictures. You'll be the only one doing so in the room.

To find out when gallery previews are is as easy as attending them. When an exhibition is about to begin, the preview will usually be the evening before. You only have to phone the gallery and say, 'I'm supposed to be going to the preview with a friend who has the invite – and just wanted to confirm the date and time.'

Alternatively, dress in your Armani or Dior and walk round Cork Street any Tuesday at 6.00 p.m.

The best way to amass a list of openings, however, is to do a quick gallery crawl, picking up all the leaflets of forthcoming exhibitions. The gallery owner will be pleased to inundate you with them, unusually helpful to the inexperienced but enthusiastic gatecrasher.

> *Once, as I was crashing the sushi restaurateur Simon Woodroffe's book launch, the author saw me reading his book. 'Wow!' he enthused, 'you're actually looking at it. We ought to hire you. You make such a good advert!'*

# Read All About It

Newspapers, television and radio relentlessly advertise free parties daily. The beginning of a festival, the opening of a new club or restaurant or hospital department, or a death will immediately alert the experienced crasher. It is then a simple matter of phoning the organisers, saying the friend you're escorting is on holiday, but you wanted to confirm the venue and time.

# The Beginner's Guide

It's worth listing, at this point, party venues in order of accessibility...

# Dangerous Places

**Hotels**

These are particularly welcoming to the gatecrasher, because, like banks, shops, or public lavatories, they are open to all. If you're smartly dressed enough you'll be greeted with inquiries about your wellbeing. Once I was prowling the corridors of the Waldorf, sporting a black tie, and was actually found and personally escorted by a waiter into a crowded ballroom for a champagne reception.

**Restaurants, Bars, Shops**
Parties held in these are easily penetrated because of the confusing fact that, usually, party guests and customers use the same lavatories. You go into the lavatory with your glass as a customer, and, miraculously transformed, like Clark Kent in his telephone kiosk, you come out as a party guest, walking straight into the function room or segregated alternative bar. The lavatory also, if you're looking for a quiet night, serves the reverse process. You take a couple of filled glasses from the party room, go to the lavatory, then take the glasses into the bar area instead, to be enjoyed in peace.

**Embassies and Government Buildings**

These share equal fourth place – with, curiously, nightclubs – because all are built to stop undesirables from entry.

The first two are understandable: you could be a Saddam Hussein sympathiser with a very loud party-popper. But don't be discouraged: you should remember the IMPOSSIBLE PARTY FALLACY (*see page 132*).

Two of my most effortless party crashes have been the American Ambassador's private residence and the VIP room of Buckingham Palace.

**Nightclubs**

The nightclub is unexpectedly difficult because, like casino operators, the management make the Machiavellian assumption that everybody is born corrupt. Nightclubs are expecting crashers. In fact, clubs almost seem designed for the sole purpose of throwing people out. The entrances of nightclubs usually only permit single file; the heavies guarding them are anxious to feel their daily workout isn't going to be wasted that evening.

The night club entrance is best approached with a group. If you are careful you can be part of that group.

Annabel's has an entrance and staircase designed for an anorexic tropical fish. I loitered round the corner until I saw a party of five approaching, and tagged on. Two officials stood at the top of the stairs with guest lists.

'Make sure everyone has their invites,' one said to the other. It was a promotion party. As my group waited in the cloakroom queue, one of them handed over an invitation card. 'There're five of us,' she said, descending the stairs. Two others followed, and I was the fourth. If the heavies (as heavies go) had above average abilities in arithmetic, it would only be a matter of time.

I needed an alibi. Entering the party room, I noticed the Easter egg of Errol Brown's head (the lead singer of Hot Chocolate).

I immediately approached him.

'Mr Brown?'

As we talked, I noticed one of the heavies just brushing passed my shoulder. He seemed to be listening to us, like a Gestapo officer listening for an English accent. We (or I) were discussing the rhyming structure of 'It Started With A Kiss'. In a few moments, the heavy lost interest, and moved on.

An ability to enter into instant conversation, incidentally, is worth cultivating. Errol Brown, in fact, seemed quite interested.

# Private Clubs

Should your brother or sister be a member of a private club and you happen to be an identical twin, you have a means of penetration. Members rapidly become known to club doormen (especially the old ones on Pall Mall – partly because the ancient doormen have been there as long as the ancient members).

However, the function rooms are often hired for award ceremonies, parties and launches. If this is the case, turn up at the appropriate time and tag on to a group. Once inside you have become a member for the night. If a more interesting party – or, even better, a formal dinner – is taking place in another room, you can join that instead.

Access to the member's notice board will offer you a diary of future events you will be able to attend as a guest.

Having said this, there are several clubs that are guarded by doormen who wouldn't react if you were an elephant, as long as you were wearing your Armani.

One club I crash so frequently that the doorman greets me, assuming I'm a member.

# What Friends Are For

You'll be surprised, with discreet and apparently casual questioning, how much free entertainment there is available.

Your first contacts will be your friends or anyone you vaguely know. Even your milkman might've heard from one of his customers or may have read about an imminent celebrity party from his *News Of The World*. Perhaps your psychiatrist is attending the Royal College of Psychiatrist's annual dinner.

Friends need subtle interrogation. Casual questioning about their employee's entertainment programmes – Christmas parties, corporate summer balls, conference dinners.

They may know other friends who're getting married or are dying. They might've gone to university and have annual reunion dinners; they may be members of the golf club. Your yoga teacher might go to weekend conferences with formal dinners and less formal parties.

## A WARNING

*One of the effects of prolonged gatecrashing, unnoticed at first, like Alzheimer's disease, is a gradual defocusing and eventual decay of moral judgement (see* THE LONELINESS OF THE LONG DISTANCE GATECRASHER page 226). *In your new pastime you'll make many friends but remember they're only party friends, and you only know them through deception.*

# The Mantelpiece

When I visit a private house – anyone's house – I don't seek out the kitchen for a drink; I go to the mantelpiece. Very few people can resist letting it be known they're popular. On most mantelpieces there's a sign which says:

> *'I really despair sometimes of my frenetic social life. This is the price, I suppose, of being so much admired.'*

The sign is subtly disguised – well, not that subtly – as a row of invitation cards. These are what you're looking for. They need to be as efficiently gutted of information as a fishmonger cleans a fish – particularly if you have to make conversation with the house owner and don't have much time. The rule is: date, location, time.

After, you can glance to see whether it's a wedding, party or court summons. Until you have a chance to use the lavatory, you'll need to commit these facts to memory.

If there's a painting above the mantelpiece you can play for extra time – particularly if the host painted it themselves and it's hideous (if hideous, they will spend longer talking about it, since no-one else would ever ask) Of course, as you listen to their discourse, you're busy memorising the invitations.

Family photos, often conveniently placed on mantelpieces, provide another good time wasting ploy while you do your research.

# The Spy Rule

The first rule of every secret service is that their operators never reveal their contacts (ideally, they wouldn't actually recognise one another even if they were sharing a bath). The worse crime a gatecrasher can commit is to use the name of a contact as a means of party entry.

This is not out of loyalty (which to the hardened gatecrasher is a meaningless word, like 'honesty' or 'generosity'), but necessity. Not only will the contact never forgive you, but to do this is professional suicide – for two reasons. The first is that you'll lose a source of information, and secondly, the contacts themselves will no longer be trusted with the information you need.

Unlike employees of MI6, I don't know of any gatecrashers who have been tortured. When at weddings and privately financed parties, however, a notice in a bookshop I once read, 'Shoplifters will be dealt with. Then the police will be called,' often runs through my mind.

# Free To Trade

There exists an international cardsharps' sign language as complex and accurate as sign language for the deaf – a series of finger arrangements on the cards and tabletop. This has the dual function of preventing cheats erroneously working against each other, and allowing them to team up temporarily against the suckers. In the same way, fellow-liggers, once identified, can provide a great opportunity for party-date trading.

However, in the same way Sinatra, photographed arm in arm with Mafia hitmen, didn't increase his chances of canonisation, it is not helpful for gatecrashers to gather in public. If one is known he or she will contaminate the others. Excessive trading also means a party can become a coven of crashers, the monopoly of which will cause the host to ensure tighter security at subsequent parties.

Yet crashers can be particularly useful when there's no-one else to speak to, and have the added advantage – provided they keep to the drinking rules of this book – of being more coherent. Remember though, wolves hunt in packs for mutual benefit, but each wolf is after the tastiest piece. (This applies, of course, to relationships of any kind.)

Ideally, though, like spies dropping a package from one to the other as they pass in the street, crashers should meet briefly over a canapé plate, then separate.

# The Conversation

One of your first aims on arrival is to be seen in animated conversation. This has two important advantages – firstly, and most importantly, it allies suspicion (be careful, though, not to pick on the guest-list arranger), and secondly, it is your first step to obtain information, information, of course, about this and future parties

Pumping the other guests for information is of particular importance at a cold crash (*a cold crash being a party or function the reason for its existence of which you haven't the faintest idea – see COLD CRASH page 102*). You are after information about the guests, but mainly the hosts and what provoked them to be so generous.

You need to know as much information about the party and the other guests as possible. By learning the names of other guests, you can subsequently drop them into other conversations, as if you know them. By learning about the party, you can enrich your own fictional biography of the evening, like an actor researching his part.

Parties are stepping-stones. One reason for going to one is to discover and leap on to the next. Once you've started on the road to professional gatecrashing, your contacts and party possibilities should increase with inevitable arithmetical progression.

Therefore, your second duty at any party (the first, of course, being to seek out the best champagne), is to gain knowledge of future parties.

# MANNERS MAKETH GATECRASHERS

In the early twenty-first century, if a man gives up his seat on the tube to a heavily pregnant, paraplegic blind octogenarian, other passengers will openly gasp at this seemingly extravagant act of courtesy. To be seen as well-mannered today gives you an aura of divinity, imbues you with an otherworldly, heart-rending purity.

There's a story by one of the Russian gloom-merchants – possibly Dostoevsky – of a gatecrasher who drops in on a wedding. As he becomes more and more drunk, he finally starts kissing the bride, accidentally causing the newly-weds to enter into a vicious and catastrophic argument.

It is a good example of how not to behave.

You must always respect your hosts, even if they're serving peanuts and Lambrusco Rosé.

# How To Be Drunk

You would expect the primary gatecrashing rule to be not to drink at all. However, to remain completely sober would be to partially defeat the purpose of your crash.

A certain alcoholic state is even helpful so that you are more in mental harmony with your other guests, more in accord with how they may see you or – depending on their level of intoxication – be oblivious to you. If the guests are sufficiently well fuelled, and have not taken their pre-party cheese wedges, they won't care who you are, especially if you're fun.

My personal rule is to drink steadily on arrival, reach a state of reasonable alcoholic fulfillment (usually reached in under an hour). Then abruptly stop: from this point on, drink only water. Apart from relaxing you, possibly making you for a while deliriously happy and affable, the distinct advantage is that at the same time as you slowly regain your sobriety, the other guests become increasingly incapable. This places you – and them – in the ideal states required to extract future party information. And the method of extraction is largely dependent on your manner.

# The Secrets Of Seduction

In Dale Carnegie's clever, if morally dubious, book *How To Win Friends and Influence People*, he pinpoints the key to being irresistible: always, always speak in term of the other person's interests. For the gatecrasher, there are important additional benefits – particularly for the Cold Crash .

One evening, passing the Mall Gallery, I noticed well-dressed people entering, and followed. A man wearing a red quasi-military tunic asked my name, so I gave one, 'Robert Langton'.

'MR ROBERT LANGTON!'

The voice boomed with the shock of a starting pistol. As I walked down the stairs, shaken by the blast, several women, all looking like cousins of the Queen, and dinner-jacketed men shook my hand. In the reception they were serving Veuve Cliquot. I noticed in the gallery itself, dinner had been set up for 200.

A universal law, as invariable and certain as gravity or the Golden Mean, is that if 100 guests are invited to dinner, at least one won't turn up, due to depression, illness, or death (or all three). I rapidly drank my champagne allowance and waited for everyone to be seated. I then sat in one of the two available seats.

Although there was someone sitting either side of me, I was only ever asked one question throughout the evening: 'Are you Lady B — ?'

(I was sitting in her seat. *See HOW TO DEAL WITH NAME-PLACES page 90.*)

Probably more than half the population in the civilized world, at some point, pay someone to listen to them talk about themselves. It's surprising, even worrying, the extent to which people can be dissuaded from asking you questions once you've convinced them your ears were created purely for their benefit. Once he'd asked his single question, I spent the rest of the evening eating poached salmon, roast duck and chocolate mousse, while Lord C offered me his complete, unexpurgated autobiography.

What he told me would've given a blackmailer an orgasm. It was information I could've done without. However, it fulfilled one of the most important requirements for gatecrasher conversation – diverting questions away from yourself.

By the time I got to leave, Lord C knew nothing more about me other than the relatively certain fact that I wasn't Lady B.

# Mr Nice

(The smile) *'understood you just as far as you wanted to be understood, believed in you as you would like to believe in yourself, and assured you that it had precisely the impression of you that, at your best, you hoped to convey.'*

This is part of the charm of Jay Gatsby, the eponymous hero of Fitzgerald's novel. Once someone discovers that you are such a person, they'll be very reluctant to leave you (even if you'd like them to). Being seen in conversation is the gatecrasher's invisibility cloak. Also, interest, intelligence, sympathy and admiration are the anesthetics of suspicion. It's possible to render the other person completely insensible with self-esteem.

# The Waiter's Waiter

Short of bowing to the host's goldfish, your courtesy should be all-inclusive. Waiters are as saturated with knowledge of future parties as the editor of *Hello* magazine. Stunned by your deference, they can be made to reveal priceless party information, even the means to penetrate them. Photographers, bar staff, the girl on the switchboard, the porter, the cleaner, the candlestick replacer – all these people have eyes and ears and know things you don't. When yoy are dressed in your Dior dress and holding a glass of golden champagne, they're flattered by your interest in them, listening to their grievances, memories of their daughter's wedding, or the cat's funeral, as you slowly prize open their information file.

Of course, this friendliness towards staff may be thought patronising. It is. You'll quickly learn, however, that the gatecrasher, like Machiavelli's prince, should discipline him or herself to avoid the affliction of moral self-questioning*.

*\* Having done my stint as a waiter after university, perhaps I have more empathy with catering staff than I pretend. At some parties, I feel envious of them, sure they're having more fun in the kitchen.*

# The Host's Host

In the animal kingdom, a parasite, as long as it does not jeopardise its own needs, will do all it can not to jeopardise its host. A parasite can even be the means of maintaining the host's health – the bird that cleans the crocodile's teeth – or even survival – the honeybee and the flower.

A bold but rewarding move can be to take the role, if needed, of a deputy host. I was near the door at a party when Lord Archer entered and stood, ill-at-ease, waiting to be greeted.

No-one approached him (and this was even before his perjury case was a mere twitch in his eye), so I stepped forward, introduced myself, and gave him a glass of champagne. Archer relaxed and became chatty.

A few minutes later a host arrived and I introduced the two. For the rest of the evening I was unchallenged, even welcomed, if only because I seemed to know Jeffrey Archer.

At another party I was chatting to a publicity girl when Lady Antonia Fraser came in. The publicity girl immediately introduced me, and then herself.

'I'm sorry', the publicity girl apologised to the new arrival, 'and your name is?'

Lady Fraser was momentarily silent – that particular silence of astonishment combined with steely outrage – then hissed her name and stalked off. An unusual case of the gatecrasher being introduced but not the invited VIP.

The next time this situation arose, I took the initiative and introduced Tom Stoppard to a publishing financial director, one of the hosts, who hadn't recognised him. I then maintained the conversation by talking to Stoppard about his work. This is another way you can be of service to yourself and your host – knowing something about important guests.

# WHO DO YOU THINK YOU'RE SPEAKING TO?

Never assume, though, familiarity, especially with celebrities. Since celebrities, by definition, are so much seen on TV and film, many people feel they are old friends if they happen to meet them in the supermarket. They slap them on the back, put their arms round them, ask them for a fiver.

When I addressed Mick Jagger as 'Mr Jagger', the formality, together with that of my suit, made him suddenly more attentive, as if the term was so unusual he wasn't at first sure who 'Mr Jagger' was. (*See STAR GAZING page 148.*)

# Being There

Successful gatecrashing, like holiday weather, comes with no guarantee. Your evening may end up on a rain-swept street, staring up at lit windows filled with happy, well-fed and intoxicated shadows. You could be faced with a house in sleep at the end of a cul-de-sac. In search of the cold crash, you're obliged to stalk the streets, checking out all the likely venues, reduced to the dreary footwork of police looking for a lead. Where you live, then, can dictate the odds of a good night out.

Living in a flat that looks out on the face of Big Ben, I'm soon in party heartland: the Square Party Mile. A quick inspection of the Festival Hall, a walk across the river to take in the National Gallery, the Crypt of St Martin's-in-the Fields, up to Brown's function rooms, then into Soho itself – Groucho's, the Soho Club, and so on, then finally to Piccadilly for the sure-bet, six-storied Café Royale. On the way home, I'll pop into The Savoy for a late corporate supper. Sometimes I even stay for the tasteless cabaret, or wait for the dispensing of corporate company's farewell gifts.

# The Hotel

For the gatecrasher searching for the Cold Crash (*see page 102*), hotels are unusually sympathetic. A special information board is generously provided for the crasher in the foyer. This lists all functions held that day, including details of the party or dinner, the corporate bodies involved, or names of the hosts, the function room in which it is to be held, and often the time at which you should consider crashing. For weddings, they are particularly helpful, because they name the couple involved. This is important since weddings are dangerous.

The two advantages of the corporate party over the private party for the gatecrasher is that at the corporate party everyone doesn't know everyone else, and no-one there has had to finance it out of their own pocket.

The reason why weddings, like funerals, are particularly dangerous is that they're financed by the Mafia – the family.

# A Double Wedding

So usually I avoid weddings. However, I was staying in a large hotel on a wet Saturday evening, and since the hotel was in Swindon, I was particularly desperate. Fortunately the ideal opportunity – the only one I'd recommend – presented itself: there were two wedding parties.

Memorising the couples' names from the gatecrasher's notice board in the foyer, I found a discarded champagne glass in the bar and wandered into the ballroom where Caroline and David were entertaining their guests. The party of 100 was well underway, the hot buffet already steaming. My glass had been refilled three times before a silver-haired man found me finishing a plate of poached salmon and asparagus. He had that military habit of standing as if he had a ceremonial sword inserted into his backside, then up the spinal column to the cerebral cortex.

'Sorry. We haven't met.'

'Robert,' I said.

'And you're with?'

'Yvonne.'

'Yvonne?'

At this point a woman joined him.

'Yes, Yvonne,' I said. 'Friend of the bride's.'

'I'm the bride.'

'I'm the bride's father.' The man now had a definite military look, the set of a thin-lipped mouth suggesting SAS experience.

'Ah. Yvonne Brightwell? She should be here soon.' I turned to the bride. 'But you must be Rebecca.'

'No, I'm Caroline.'

'What?' I put down my glass. 'This *is* Rebecca and Sebastian's party?'

The Gulf War veteran barked out what sounded like an order for a firing squad, momentarily paralysing me, until I realised it was supposed to be a laugh.

'You're at the wrong wedding, man. There's two on tonight. You should probably be at the other.'

'I'm so sorry. I do apologise. I feel awful.'

'Don't worry. Easy mistake. Have another glass of champers before you go. Better than the stuff next door, I bet, eh?'

I did take a fourth glass, if only out of relief that the commander of the British Forces in Bosnia had taken my error so generously. Then, with the glass, I descended the stairs to the second wedding.

I stayed at this one for the rest of the evening, never needing to explain I was supposed to be at David and Caroline's wedding.

# On Leaving

Keeping to the rule that you've stopped drinking, and your curtain of alcoholic mist has risen while everyone else is ambulating in thick fog, you should take the opportunity to leave – if you're sober enough, you'll be glad to.

The last rule of gatecrasher's etiquette is that you should always leave early so as to give people time to forget you were ever there.

# THE MAGIC DOOR

The door is the borderline crossing, Check Point Charlie. It's like customs and you've got a kilo of pure Bolivian cocaine taped painfully round your stomach. If you get past the door, many – possibly all – your problems are over. There are a number of techniques to gain entry, and each situation demands instant analysis and a strategy. One of the attributes of successful generals is their ability to prepare elaborate and detailed battle plans, and, in the war zone, due to unforeseen circumstances, to be flexible enough to instantly abort them, and to evolve a completely different strategy.

If at all possible, do all you can to avoid the guest-list check. Avoidance is possible by the following method: look as if you are already there.

For this you'll now appreciate why you need thermal underwear. The advantage of this is that you are not hampered by the possibly fatal delay at the cloakroom. The second reason is that you look like someone who's already arrived, someone who's just gone to make a mobile phone call or have a pee. This alone is often enough to allow you to sweep past the heavily clad guests waiting for their cloakroom tickets and gathered round the guest-list official. This can be further enhanced by waving to someone in the party room as you approach.

> *A further, effective flourish is to bring your own wine or champagne glass. Remove this discreetly from your pocket or bag, then your resemblance to a guest returning to the party is instantly complete.*

On arrival, wait out of sight, if possible, or loiter, looking at your watch, as if expecting someone. When a sizable group of guests enter, tag on. As they surround the guest-list official, you wait at the back, until the former is absorbed in search of obscure names. As the guests, checked off, begin to wander in, you slip in amongst them.

## CRITICAL MASS

Arrival time at a party is critical. You must seek entry at THE MOMENT OF MAXIMUM STAMPEDE. It's no use arriving 20 minutes too early or too late only to find yourself facing four or five languishing officials with nothing better to do than a thorough credential check – perhaps even a strip search for good measure.

# Are You Paying Attention?

One of G.K.Chesterton's Father Brown stories – 'The Invisible Man' – is about a murder in a house that is closely watched. No-one is seen entering or leaving. The postman did it. The reasoning behind his invisibility is that postmen are so accepted, like traffic noise or street bins – they are not noticed. Their presence is only subliminally registered. (In fact, postmen are only noticed when you want to complain about their absence.)

No matter how hard a person concentrates, there will come a moment, a point of inattention: the moment when you crash your new TVR, drop a Ming vase, forget the name of someone who's just introduced themselves, a little point when the mind slips into the sea of an alien planet and then slips back. (Interestingly, the greater your concentration, the more profound, when it comes, is this moment.)

Being able to identify that moment in another person is the magician's greatest secret. It's not so much a technique, as a sensibility: if mastered, it is the closest a human being can come to possessing supernatural powers. You can perform literal miracles. Uri Geller, exploiting this single ability, became a multi-millionaire. For the gatecrasher, it's the best method of getting past the door.

The POINT OF INATTENTION method is essential – and at it's most elegant – for theatre, opera, and concert crashing (*see ENTERING THE TWILIGHT ZONE page 162*). Although used differently for parties, the principle is the same.

Since the phenomenon is used as a conjurer's device, the easiest way to demonstrate it is by describing the most obvious – as well as most tedious – of magician's gambits: picking a card. A choice is made and you return the card to the deck. You're watching it as if you'd given the magician a £50 note. There is no way you'll relinquish your eyes from the pack. The magician shuffles and squares the cards, ready to begin the trick. Just before he does, as if an afterthought, he says, 'Oh, you did memorise it, didn't you?'

Your eyes flick up momentarily to say 'Yes', then immediately flick down. You won't remember your eyes ever leaving the pack – but you're too late. The card you chose is no longer in the pack.

Arriving at the venue, you stand patiently a little away from the reception desk or party door. As you check your watch, it's clear you're waiting for your partner. The official, suspicious at first, will watch you, even as the other guests arrive. As the guests continue to file in, culminating in the Moment Of Maximum Stampede, you glance at your watch more frequently, your expression puzzled. The official still watches you, but is more engrossed in ticking his or her list as people begin to queue. Then something minor happens: a guest trips; another finds themselves not on the list; someone can't find the lavatory; a car backfires, a canapé waiter farts. Something will happen creating the Moment Of Inattention.

You slip through the door because by this time you've become invisible.

You are a postman.

# The Guest-List Con

A combat soldier will finally have to face live ammunition; you'll eventually have to take the guest-list head on. It is possible to find your name on the list by use of an elegant method employed by conjurers for certain bogus memory feats. It requires boldness, and a sharp eye, but if executed smoothly, is convincing.

You approach the guest-list official (who should be at least moderately busy). You mumble a bland name beginning with a letter from the latter end of the alphabet – but nothing offbeat like Ustinov or Zebedee. You must position yourself so that you can read the list with the official (if he or she keeps it to his or herself you're sunk). You join him helpfully in the search for your name.

What you're really doing is finding another name (one that's unticked and of your sex).

When the official reaches where your name should be there's a chance it actually will be there, or one sounding similar enough for him to think he misheard you. When it's not there, you look suitably surprised.

'That's odd. I RSVP'd weeks ago.'

'Doesn't seem to be here, sir.'

'Funny – oh, unless they've used my working name. I'm a journalist.'

'And that name is, sir?'

You then give the name you've just picked out. The official, eager not to have a confrontation, will be as relieved as you are to find it there.

For a female crasher, the excuse of a married and working name is even more plausible.

Ensure, before using this method, that you're not crashing a Magic Circle's anniversary dinner.

# Yes, My Name Is Tom Cruise

## How To Pick Up A Name Badge

Generally, all gatecrashing procedure, like murder or petty theft, is best done without hesitation. The name badge must be picked up boldly, so quickly, in fact, that no one – not even you – has time to register the name. It could be the name of someone of the opposite sex; it could be the name of a guest's pet dog. You just say, 'Ah, there I am,' then walk on, appearing to pin the badge to your jacket.

Of course, you'll never actually wear it. (If later challenged, you say you didn't want to damage your jacket – if it costs what it should, you won't. You then produce the badge, waving it so that the name is unreadable, saying, 'But don't worry, I've got it here.')

Often, being checked off the guest list and receiving your name badge is a simultaneous procedure. If so, you're in luck since it means the guest list, in the form of badges, is now displayed in at least 15-point print all over the table top.

As guests gather round the table, you approach, your eye immediately seizes on a name, which you then give to the official. You then both hunt for the name badge, as if you haven't yet looked.

# Yes, My Name Is Prince Charles

## How To Deal With Name-Places

A champagne reception before dinner, however tempting, is best avoided until towards the end. The champagne has slipped mercilessly through the guests' empty stomachs, and, swift as a vampire, straight to the veins. If at this point you enter, you appear to be merely returning, like others, from the loo. Take a couple of glasses – one for your partner – and, after a few moments, leave the room looking for him or her.

## RECONNAISSANCE

During your brief time in the reception room it's advantageous to inspect the seating plan to gain information about the guests, the corporate bodies involved, and – the Crasher's Haven – spare seats for unexpected arrivals. Perusal of the plan serves also to make you look credibly occupied.

As you sip your champagne in the stress-free privacy of the hotel bar, you wait for the guests to be seated. You'll know when this moment has arrived. You'll hear giggling, clinking of glasses from the reception room as the waiters judge the remaining champagne in a corner, with their feet up. You walk into the dining room where wine and first course are being served. No-one will be looking at you since by this time they'll be in a mild state of starvation and will be looking at their smoked salmon. The spare seats will stick out like missing incisors from Leo di Caprio's mouth.

You must choose a seat immediately, as if you know where you're going. As you sit, your neighbours will either smile or look confused, depending on whether the seat is meant to be occupied by a colleague or a stranger.

In either case, you must say, 'No, I am not Madonna' (or whoever's name is written on your place card). 'The trouble is I've been put next to my ex- partner/a creditor/an employee I recently sacked/an Ordnance Survey Map collector.'

Another very effective excuse, gaining immediate compassion, is to say your partner is ill, even better, is in hospital, so you're on your own and 'feeling a little lonely'. You then continue: 'I was wondering if I could sit here instead. If Madonna turns up I can easily move. You don't even have to talk to me.'

Usually they're pleased. Your immediate neighbours prefer an alternative to speak to (their other neighbour may be an Ordnance Survey Map collector) – especially someone so willing to listen to them. If it is a corporate bought seat, after all, it would only otherwise be wasted.

Never say you are the name on the card. Even if your neighbours wouldn't know you from Madonna, Madonna might turn up.

# Sitting Uncomfortably

The most dangerous person to sit next to is the party organiser or the host, both of whom may be the same person. This happened to me at a Dental College annual reunion dinner, when the only two seats happened to be next to the Dean of the Faculty. I mention this incident partly as it initiated a curious exchange.

'You look a bit lost,' he said.

'Well, I am a bit. I'm meant to be here with my wife, but we've had an argument. That's why I'm late. I'm hoping she'll still turn up.'

'Which year were you?'

'Oh, it's my wife who's the dentist, not me.'

'What's her name?'

I thought of a dental student I knew at university. 'Docherty.'

'You mean Doughty.'

'That's right.'

'Which one?'

'Which one?'

'Younger or older?'

'Oh. Younger.'

For the rest of the evening we talked teeth (or was it his Ordnance Survey Map collection?). What struck me as curious, however, was that the Dean showed no suspicion of the fact that I was ignorant of my wife's name.

It is a good example of how, if, like the cardsharp, you're not otherwise suspected, you can afford to fumble the odd card. It also demonstrates the effectiveness of the pre-prandial drinks reception.

Innocence dulls the watcher's concentration like ether. Uri Geller's wide-eyed earnestness dares you to question his otherwise dubious miracles. Once I crashed a formal dinner and talked to a couple who later became friends. When I finally confessed my evening profession, they couldn't believe I'd crashed the dinner where I'd met them.

'But your name was on the place card,' they claimed. My apparent innocence was such that they were convinced they had read my name on the card. The dinner was in Inner Temple: the couple were extremely successful criminal barristers.

# Who Are You?

This question should be one you ask yourself every time you don your Armani or Dior, check your black bow tie, and run through your accessories. At a cold crash, of course, the question can only be asked when you discover why the party is being held. However, like Blood Group O, in an emergency, a job that is universally accepted at most parties, is that of a free-lance journalist. As the evening progresses, though, you should be elaborating in your mind, as well as your conversation, as your party knowledge increases.

In my incarnation as a cardiac consultant, I have sometimes reached the point of elaboration at which I am tempted – when guests ask – to offer advice. So far, though, I have resisted.

In *Wall Street*, Bud Fox (Charlie Sheen), watching the midnight skyline from the balcony of his penthouse flat, earned through shady dealings, asks 'Who Am I?', the only philosophical inquiry in the film. Unfortunately, it's an inquiry brought prematurely to a close as soon as he's asked the question. As your gatecrashing career flourishes, however, this question will be one you increasingly ask yourself – and one, if you wish to retain a modicum of integrity, you should keep asking.

# The Cardsharp's Rule

The cardsharp can only effectively operate if he isn't closely watched. In this way, he can afford to be less skillful in card manipulation than the conjurer (although he has to perform sleights at the table, which affords little cover and demands minimum hand and arm movement.).

For this reason, the cardinal Cardsharp's Rule is that at the least suspicion, he must immediately leave. It is also the gatecrasher's. As your experience grows, you'll develop a sixth sense telling you when you're in danger. Clyde Barrow, Bonnie's partner, had an uncanny ability to sense a police trap and so avoid them. The one time he neglected to trust his intuition, he made a sudden, painful – if briefly realised – discovery that he had more than a hundred machine-gun bullets lodged in most parts of his anatomy.

Not to obey the Cardsharp's Rule is to invite disaster. Trust it, as really you've little to lose. It's only a party.

# The Shoplifter's Rule

The majority of shoplifters are caught because they keep coming back to the same shop. Store detectives start looking out for them warmly, like Savile Row tailors look out for faithful customers. If you've crashed the British Wood Pulp 86th Anniversary Dinner at the Savoy on Wednesday, try the Park Lane hotels for the remainder of the week. The hosts might be different but the officials and waiters aren't.

They might wonder at your daily career changes.

# Thoughts

## to help you on your way through the door

**1** Party hosts – particularly those holding formal dinners, balls, gala lunches etc. – are not really expecting gatecrashers, especially if they are immaculately dressed. (For many film previews, a black tie often serves as an alternative invitation card.) If it's a formal dinner with place-names, there is even less concern, since, theoretically, a gatecrasher would have nowhere to sit.

**2** People, especially in England, have a horror of possible hostile confrontation. Officials are anxious not to offend important guests; like most employees, they want as few problems as possible, and an early night.

**3** When you have a party yourself, your biggest fear is that no-one's going to show.

# THE COLD CRASH

You've been dropped in the jungle with a packet of diarrhoea pills and a paper tissue, and you have to find your way home. Snakes, spiders and, since you're in enemy territory, malign but intelligent life are lurking, looking for a kill.

With the Cold Crash you're equally vulnerable to capture, often less adequately equipped. Success is dependent on your abilities of assimilation and acclimatisation, of picking up clues – the equivalent of finding a river source, identifying an enemy camp, getting your bearings from the sky.

# Cold Crash Tactics

Although this is largely intuitive, the following are helpful hints:

**1** Welcome placards saying, for instance, 'Amy's 50th', or 'Coutt's Bank Ball'; any literature on side tables; discarded invitation cards (pick up and pocket, in case of being challenged later); dinner menus on the tables; a seating-plan.

**2** The conversation. Often the nature of the party can be surmised by the type and contents of the conversation – whether guests are talking about their race horses or their racing-pigeons, whether they have trouble paying the mortgage or having to live on the Isle of Man. Clothes, too, will often indicate not only financial position but also the wearer's aesthetic judgement, often a barometer of social and professional status. A patterned tie with a patterned shirt, a dress just a little too pink, an overdose of jewelry – you are at a moderately successful accountant's annual bash.

## HINT
*If most of the guests are in their early nineties, carefully negotiating each other's wheelchairs, it may not a Spice Girls' promotion party.*

**3** An important and helpful observation is to notice if guests seem to know each other or not. If the former, begin to look confused, since very soon you'll be approached and will be obliged, if challenged, to say, 'This is Simon's leaving party?' Against all odds, it might be.

At this point it is worth describing two cold crashes – one bad, one good – to demonstrate some of the techniques you've now learnt, and how they are actually utilised in the field.

# The Bad Crash

Following a false trail to a West Kensington address, I found myself without a party and too far from the Square Party Mile. Like a deprived addict, I craved a fix. Addiction, although making you bolder and more ruthless, can also interfere with your crashing intuition – even override it.

As soon as I saw the shop with the surrounding pavement cordoned off with rope, and the three men in black, sporting shades and mobiles, I felt myself preparing for a *kamikaze* mission. I walked straight past and hid round a corner. I ate an egg contemplatively. Well-dressed couples, fanning large invitation cards, were ascending steps up to the four-floor glass shop, on each floor of which I could see the champagne trays floating.

The evening was warm with an apricot light, lending the champagne a duskier, honeyed colour, urging me forward.

The Moment of Maximum Stampede was approaching, so I needed to make a strike soon, or not at all. Walking back up the street on the heavies' blind side, I let a shoal of guests overtake me, then tagged on. I closed up on them as we approached the entrance, and just as we did so, I said,

'Just in time! Couldn't park the car.'

'We had the same problem,'said the girl near me. 'We found one at the back.'

'That's where I went in the end.'

By the time this absorbing conversation had ended, invitation cards had been flashed, I felt myself climbing stairs, and then the sudden relief of a cool glass in my hand.

As my new friends were greeted, I wandered discreetly away, like smoke does from a campfire on a still evening. I climbed more stairs, searching for the equivalent of foliage cover – a concentration of guests. Why was someone having a party in a posh, clothes shop? I didn't – and never would have – recognised Paul Smith, but Paul Smith seemed to recognise an Armani suit. As I reached the top floor, I heard a girl describing the range of some exclusive toys in their children's section. It was gradually becoming apparent it wasn't so much a party in a shop as a party for the shop: I was at a shop launch. As this dawning permeated my conscious, a trim, middle-aged man, simply but well dressed, with kind, thoughtful eyes put out a hand.

'I'm sorry. And you are?'

'Robert. And you?'

'Me? I'm Paul. Paul Smith. My party.'

'I do apologise.'

'Don't worry.'

'Fantastic shop. Actually, I was looking at the suits.'

'Try one. Let me find someone who can help.'

There was something not quite right, a feeling you might have if someone was stalking you. Even when I was being shown a variety of suits and enjoyed an animated discussion with the young assistant hoping for promotion, I couldn't help thinking someone was watching me, someone who had seen me enter.

Concluding our conversation about suits, his promotion, future, whether he really wanted to move in with his girlfriend Miriam, who lived in Balham, but was originally from Hassocks, I left the assistant and found myself with a man in a business suit and a dull tie.

It was now I noticed I'd seen him when I came in: was it his eyeballs that had seared the back of my neck? They were dark and penetrating, like Kafka's. I could tell I was in trouble when I couldn't deflect the conversation, no matter how much I enthused about the shop, the party, his tie. It was like a hopeless boxing match: each time I took a swipe, he ducked, and followed through with a direct hit.

His questions too, had an uncanny knack of being the very ones I always seek to avoid. Who was I? How did I know Sarah who I was with, the one I said who had the invitation? Why did she have an invitation?

Obviously at this point I should have left, but I urgently needed one more glass of champagne.

Briefly excusing himself, the Suit wandered over to an assistant, who disappeared down stairs, while he returned. Although he let me ask questions now, it was he who disconcertingly held me in conversation – until one of the men in black arrived, still wearing his shades.

'Could we see your invitation, sir?'

'My partner Sarah's got it. She's still trying to park the car, I think.'

It wasn't so much the tone of voice as the simple inarguable forefinger curl informing me to follow him off the premises that wounded me so much.

Fortunately, the guests on the two floors we had to descend were too drunk to notice my chaperoned departure. They might have even thought I was so important I needed an escort to ensure a rapid exit. This, however, didn't assuage my humiliation.

Sometimes, on the few occasions this has happened, I wonder if it's damaged professional pride that depresses me, or is it really the idea of not being wanted? Stepping out into the still sunlit street, I said,

'It'll be okay if we come back with the invitation, won't it?'

He nodded with total disbelief, making me feel worse.

The story has a surprising twist. Promising myself never to ever contemplate crashing a party again – more, to live my life virtuously, like I did at school; never to lie or take anything without paying for it, never allowing myself to even say something I don't genuinely mean – I caught a bus to Charing Cross, crossed the bridge, and dropped in on the Festival Hall for a pee. In the lower atrium, a private party was well underway.

Immediately, in a reflex action, I skipped down the stairs, took a glass of Australian red, and noticed a woman who smiled. She said,

'Are you a gatecrasher?'

'Hardly,' I smiled back, 'I'm in general charge of administration here.'

The party was an end of conference celebration for a corporate firm; she too had an administrative position and had helped organise this event. She confided, later, she hated her job and envied mine of working at the Festival Hall. She asked if there were any similar positions coming up, and insisted that I take her details. Her friendliness extended to fetching me another glass of wine, and a lift home.

As we left the party, both warmed by each other's fortuitous meeting, and stepped into the relaxing seats of her corporate Mercedes, I felt a renewal of faith, a trust in the human heart. Trust, honesty: isn't it that what it's really all about?

# The Good Cold Crash

I was on my way to a nothing-else-on-that-night crash (a Mechanical Engineers Reunion dinner). The sun was now level with Hungerford Bridge. I loitered on the centre of the bridge, enjoying some roast turkey I'd found at a party the previous night. The flute player was packing up, off to the Festival Hall for his wash and pee before kipping down on the embankment. Three city workers with briefcases and *Evening Standards,* were talking to their mobiles. 'I'm on Hungerford Bridge,' two of them said, the third asking what was for dinner.

The *Big Issue* man with the ponytail, glasses and undaunted cheerfulness had already gone. The evening sightseeing ferry was swinging towards the landing stage, its windows a series of gold spangles, each a setting sun. As I watched it, I noticed a larger boat already moored, and on the middle deck people were drinking. This wasn't unusual, except all of them held the same drink – champagne.

From the bridge, I had a pigeon's eye view of the landing stage. Two heavies with lists inspected the invitation cards. Once checked off, guests walked further down the stage to the single-file gangway up into the boat. From my vantage point, it was like looking at a plan of a maze. I could see a way of by-passing the heavies, provided they were distracted.

First I had to get on to the landing stage by posing as one of the tourists boarding the sightseeing ferry. The use of an old Royal Garden Party technique told to me by a veteran ligger seemed appropriate, the principle of which is to go through the exit as people are leaving, claiming you've left your umbrella/husband/child/cat.

Soon I was getting my sea legs on the landing and edging my way slowly beyond the vision of the heavies, as if I was waiting for a boat. I was soon behind them, on their left; the gangway entailed a 15-metre walk across open space.

The Moment Of Inattention came quicker than
I'd expected. A flock of guests made me move, in a
kind of hurried stroll (a difficult feat), until I'd joined
the first of the party. Together we filed down the
gangway into the darkness of the hull.

Almost simultaneously, I picked up a glass of
champagne and a name-
badge. A jazz band played
'Sweet Georgia Brown' as
smoked salmon canapés
were served.

As you would with your king in
chess, it is imperative when gatecrashing to ensure
an escape route from the outset. I was apprehensive
about finding myself up river without an excuse;
perhaps they might hand me over to the river police
– or simply throw me overboard.

A waiter told me the boat would not cast off until 8.00 p.m., so I relaxed, seeking a moment of solitude on the outer deck to savour the champagne – and learn what the party was about.

Up on Hungerford Bridge a tourist took a photo of us; a last flush of sunlight placed fine gold lines, like the edges of expensive invitation cards, on each wavelet. I found myself joining someone else on their own, sipping orange-juice, a man with receding hair and Clark Kent glasses, wearing a modest suit and a hopeful expression on his face, the hopefulness of company.

'Are you an accountant too?' he asked.

'Aren't we all?'

'I'm not actually an accountant. I work for some. Clerical. But, for long service they let me come. Did you come last year?'

'I couldn't make it last year.'

'I've been looking forward to this since Christmas, actually.'

The idea that a party which I'd casually crashed being so precious to others made me feel ungrateful and spoilt. I felt an obligation to keep him company. We went back inside and I become so engaged in conversation, and champagne, that I didn't hear, or feel, the throbbing engines. When I finally gazed out of the window, the view had changed. My Rolex read 7.30. I remembered the waiter had been Italian; he'd been on European time.

The clerk told me the boat was heading for the Dome, a long journey. Deciding to move before the clerk introduced me too soon to friends, I chatted to the hired magician. Then I went below deck to discover a dining room; tables were set with white clothes, on which stood bottles of claret, already uncorked. I was considering how I might, if there were name-places, be spending the next two or three hours in the lavatory. I considered the life-belts tied to the railings; perhaps I could jump ship, or insist on being returned to dry land owing to extreme seasickness. The engine seemed to change gear. Outside, in the now chilly last rays of sunlight, the Dome gleamed hopefully, huge and engulfing, but as delicate as the hollow egg it was, poised to blow away but for a spider's web of wire. A voice on the deck above called: 'Dinner is served.'

I rushed to the loo, but not before I saw the steaming silver buffet trays at the far end of the dining room, and the absence of name-pla ces on the tables. It was a free-for-all.

By the second course – roast lamb and a good Australian Shiraz – I had become my accountant in Milton Keynes. One of the fortunate things about people of the same profession congregating – particularly a profession as intensely fascinating as accountancy – is that no-one wants to talk about it. After watching the magician nudge a stack of two-pence pieces through the table top with a pencil, my neighbours talked to me about their children, their holiday plans: one discussed a novel she was writing.

'Do you know George?' she asked suddenly.

'No, my wife does, but she couldn't come.' I said. 'Which one is he?"

'Over there. The one with the glasses.'

Now I knew who to avoid: George, the director of an insolvency firm used by the accountants present: George, the host.

In the twilight, St Paul's – the other dome – was a silhouette, a signpost that we were nearly home. The boat was slowing down. By then, I was quite happy to stay, as were my new friends, but I knew I shouldn't linger. As I discreetly stepped towards the lowered gangway, however, a hand touched my shoulder, a light touch, but even a policeman can have a light touch.

'Excuse me.' It was George, but George was smiling. 'Have you got your present?'

'Oh! Almost forgot.'

He handed me a heavy rectangular box, ornately wrapped with gold ribbon, from a stack on a table. (At breakfast the next morning I opened it, finding a beautiful silver cigar-fat pen engraved with the firm's name.) I thanked George for the evening and the present, and walked back across Hungerford Bridge in the chilly darkness. By the steps, cross-legged and wrapped in a blanket like a squaw, was the boy with the dog.

'Any change?' the words as automatic as breathing.

Feeling I'd had a lucky night, I gave him some. It occurred to me how someone like him would truly benefit from gatecrashing more than me. A Savoy five-course dinner would sustain him for a week. If only he knew that unlimited food and drink was available, only metres away.

Even in my amoral confusion, I appreciated how things were wrong. I remembered the half-filled buffet trays left uneaten: salmon steaks and chicken breasts going cold in their sauces, whole Black Forest Gâteaux but for a slice removed, full bottles of uncorked wine standing on the tables.

As I walked the short distance home, suddenly cold and tired, I thought, if ever I become destitute, the one thing I'll hang on to is my Armani suit.

# Glittering Prizes

Award ceremonies are not necessarily a gatecrasher's delight. It's a disappointing truth that the majority of award bashes are financed by the partygoers. Producers of nominated films, or publishers of literary awards, aren't sitting at those dinner tables for fun: it's business as usual. It's a form of advertising and they pay for every seat, every glass of champagne, every black olive. Consequently, if you sat at one of their tables it wouldn't take the producer long (unless the champagne reception had been especially lavish) to guess you shouldn't be. It would be like a stranger turning up at the family breakfast table.

There are several solutions to this problem.
**1**  Find the Press Table. This will be the only table in which seats will be bought individually by the different newspapers. If there's a spare seat, you're in luck.

**2**  Sometimes, instead of a sit-down dinner, a hot buffet is served. Not only can you eat this standing up – as many do, so they can deal simultaneously – but there are usually spare tables so that guests can congregate briefly over their charcoal-grilled tuna, then return to their own tables for their raspberry bavarois and rum sauce.

**3**  Stay only for the champagne reception and canapés. This has an overwhelming advantage, and possibly, if they knew what you were intending, you would be the envy of more than half the guests, the advantage being you will probably only miss a mediocre dinner and certainly the whole of Sir Richard Attenborough's thank-you speech.

# On Being Caught

From my first few days in infant school I've developed an acute and neurotic fear of being told off. I was, for a time, so good at school, I became a touchstone of behaviour. To the other children I was a kind of pre-adolescent agony uncle, implicitly trusted; teachers often referred to me as an example of moral excellence.

Once, looking for something in my coat pocket, hanging in the cloakroom, I accidentally searched the pocket of a new boy's coat next to it. The owner accused me of stealing.

'He wouldn't do that', the others said immediately and dismissively, contemptuous of the boy's ignorance.

Perhaps my need to be loved and accepted is, after all, as great as everyone else's.

It may seem perverse for someone so terrified of punishment to indulge in a pastime inviting disgrace. (I suppose I could have chosen worse: rape, murder, loitering outside infant schools.) But if part of the thrill of gatecrashing lies in the excitement of deception, it's also the thrill, or relief, of not getting told off.

Being caught can be a humiliating experience if inadequately dealt with.

When it happens it should be treated as you would a wound – localise the damage as soon as possible, clean up the area, disinfect, and neatly dress it. This is achieved in the following ways:

The best method is to create doubt. Where this is impossible, then an instant admission that you have clearly mistaken the party for another is the safest gambit. Apologise. Your offer to pay for the wine and canapés you've consumed will, of course, be refused, but appreciated.

Having emphasised the importance of politeness, at a party of a popular novelist I was bluntly asked, as I picked up a third glass of champagne,

'Excuse me, have you been invited to this party?'

I sensed, rather than saw, the woman's tensed shoulders, but I did see the flood of blood in her cheeks, the sign of someone looking for a skirmish. Unfortunately, so was I. I was feeling unnaturally depressed that evening (even party pariahs get depressed), wondering if I wanted a party at all, or just a quiet drink on my own.

'Yes,' I said, without any attempt, or even thought, of explanation.

'And your name is?'

I gave one.

'And you were invited?'

'Yes,' I said, my cheeks, I felt, beginning to match hers, as had my tone of voice. She considered this, paused, then turned away.

Later it occurred to me that, had I really been invited, I might have reacted in exactly the same way, and perhaps this made her believe the mistake was hers.

I wouldn't normally recommend anger, though: it tends to make your challenger even more persistent, possibly abusive, possibly violent.

# IMPOSSIBLE PARTY FALLACY

'If a professional can't do it, I don't see how you expect to,' said George, a friendly ligger at a teacher's conference pre-dinner drinks reception.

'Yes, but you're talking about a professional gunman, not a professional gatecrasher.'

# The Book Launch

Salman Rushdie's book launch was receiving the full treatment by the publicity department, who would not disclose the venue until the last moment. This would seem as much a publicity manoeuvre as a precaution, but it's the kind of thing which can make the sensitive gatecrasher despondent. (I spend an inordinate amount of time each day planning – 'planning' here being another word for 'worrying about' – my entry to the evening's party.) By the time the call came through from my contact, I'd decided I definitely wouldn't go.

Waiting on the other side of the road of the Whitechapel Gallery, I saw a police van with policeman loitering about it. At the entrance were two heavies, equipped with the usual mobiles. Further inside was a table where a second set of officials held the fort. The opening scene in *Where Eagles Dare*, where Richard Burton inspects, with binoculars, a fortress he and his intrepid team have to penetrate, came to mind.

Whatever it is that drives me to spend my evenings with strangers pushed me over the road.

Indian marketsellers with plastic bags from Kwiksave trekked homewards; a couple of workmen came out of a pub; some city lawyers appeared from the tube. I'd noticed a likely group of guests further up the street, and waited for them. Two of the policemen were sitting in the van drinking coffee; another chatted with them through the open door.

Following the guests, we walked straight past the police, past the heavies, and, as the others encircled the reception table, I walked on through the Magic Door. A cold white wine was offered to me, and quail's eggs, each one individually dyed in powder blue, yellow or pink. On stands were stacked glass plates, each stack with its own dish: smoked salmon; charcoal-grilled tuna; duck salad; chicken; feta cheese. Giant white salad bowls were filled with cherry tomatoes on the vine.

The danger that the fatwa still imposed was only made evident by Rushdie himself. Standing behind him, I decided it was time for a chat.

'Mr Rushdie?'

Just for a moment, the sleepy-looking eyes, due to the owl-hoods of his eyelids, flicked open, the muscles of his neck sharpened: a flinch of

momentary fear. Just for a second Death had entered the room. (Curiously I'd seen the same reaction from another famous writer, Martin Amis, soon after he'd had all his teeth expensively capped. He probably thought I was a feminist and his dental work was at risk.)

It was a good party and a good example of the Impossible Party Fallacy.

# BAFTA Crashing

As someone who makes up fictions, as well as spending their recreational hours doing much the same, I suppose I should've guessed that other people do it too. On one occasion I was actually invited to the BAFTA awards as a TV series based on a book of mine had been nominated.

(There is little, incidentally, more galling for the crasher than to be invited to a prestigious party only to discover it could be just as easily crashed. In fact, being invited to any party inevitably leads to disappointment since there is no edge, no sense of achievement, except that of being, for once, invited. To paraphrase Groucho Marx: I wouldn't want to go to a party which would have me as a guest.)

Among the instructions sent with my invitation was that the card must be brought 'as security will be very tight' – exactly as you'd expect it to be, exactly as BAFTA's security management expected you to expect it to be. Outside the doors of the Hilton, barriers were positioned, behind which the cameras were already flickering, lending a convincing air of being impregnable. Walking straight through the entrance, I was shown the stairs to the reception room where champagne was being served. At no point did I show my invitation: there was no security. It was a bluff.

Perhaps it's a well-kept secret of the security industry that where reputation for tight security is expected, you do not actually need any security at all. The reputation is the security, in the same way a prizefighter will automatically instil fear in his opponent. It's a case of The Wizard of Oz.

## POINTLESS EXERCISE

I've wasted hours formulating ingenious strategies for crashing a particularly difficult party, only to discover no-one guarding the gate. This is so irritating that I've often felt compelled to insist on some kind of official presence to try out my technique – and to prevent further riff-raff from entering.

Perhaps the prime proof of the Fallacy is the ease with which it is possible to meet royalty. Here, security seems as antiquated, unfocused and largely absent as the Queen Mother.

On the three times I have done this – talking to Princess Anne, the Queen and Prince Philip – I've found extreme difficulty in finding any security at all. On the first occasion, at an award ceremony, I walked past the reception desk as if I lived on the premises as a resident, and talked to Princess Anne over a glass of wine, like family.

At an evening reception at the Palace (to which I *was* invited), a special room (the White Room) was reserved for VIPs, in this case about ten people. I merely stepped into the room and, to avert the suspicion of an official, immediately made conversation with one of the VIPs. In fact, I was second in line to meet the Queen. It's likely that, since the number of VIPs was so small, she would have been briefly informed about each.It says something of her poise that, on my initiating a conversation concerning a book I'd written about her called *The Queen's Knickers*, she showed no surprise or confusion. It made me think, if only her face weren't plastered on every stamp, banknote and coin, she would have had the makings of a gatecrasher.

# The Garden Party Trap

However, crashing the Palace itself is a different matter. Since those heady days when anyone could wander into the Queen's bedroom in the early morning and wake her up for a heart-to-heart, security has tightened like a python's grip. Even the innocuous Garden Party is lethal.

The Garden Party, on the face of it, has everything going for the crasher. The security forces have a real problem because of the ridiculously lengthy guest list. (There are so many garden parties, so many guests, it is becoming a rarity to meet someone who hasn't been invited). To tick names off a list as the guest arrive would be as hopeless as trying to count the bees in a swarm. With just two policemen at the gates, you'd expect to saunter through as easily as Prince Philip. The sentries in their boxes just seem for show.

The police however, do need to see something –
a little card with a name and number. This card
comes with your invitation and is the more
important of the two. You need to have access to
one to make a copy on your friend's computer.

Provided you wait for the Moment Of Maximum
Stampede – which in this case will be continuous for
about an hour – it would not be closely inspected,
even if you were invited

At least that's what you think...

However, as the thieves lurking in the pyramids
discovered, even if you manage to enter, there are
hidden trapdoors, walls that compress, pits liberally
lined with pointy sticks and a colony of bored
snakes. There are mechanisms you don't know
about, mechanisms you can't see.

Your forged card will be treated with the same light-heartedness as would the discovery in the vicar's basement of a printing press and a clothes' line full of drying banknotes.

Instead of tea in the marquee, you might be lucky to get a cup at Charing Cross Police Station as you empty your pockets and answer questions. You've committed a criminal offence. You may shortly meet, if not royalty, a peer, in the form of Jeffrey Archer.

I offer this information, not as a method, but as a warning never to try it.

Believe me. I speak with near conviction.

# The VIP Room

If you've crashed a major award ceremony, like the **BAFTA** or *Evening Standard* Play Awards, you'll have little difficulty infiltrating the VIP room.

This is simply because you have changed from being one of the suspect riff-raff outside trying to catch a glimpse of stars as they walk the red carpet: now you are a trusted guest. You're no longer the sort of person who'd think of stepping into the VIP room if you weren't supposed to be there. Security is surprisingly lax.

At one such ceremony at the Hilton, a yellow card was needed to enter the stars' exclusive reception room. An official collected the cards as the VIP and Press entered. The cards were then stacked carefully on a table. I stood nearby with a glass of champagne, waiting patiently for the Moment Of Inattention. Then I put down the glass, picked up a card, gave it back to the official, and walked in, finding myself instantly in conversation with Jamie Oliver, the TV cook.

In First Class airport lounges there is a full complimentary bar, newspapers, and a variety of snacks. Having crashed this successfully, you might still feel deprived – as the healthy gatecrasher always does feel – when you see the inner sanctum, known as the Diamond Club (a VVIP room). Again, already being a trusted passenger, getting into the Diamond Clubroom is so simple you can almost fall into it. Entry is by means of a swipe card. As you stand by the glass door, searching for your card, other VVIPs open the door with their cards. You take out your semi-hidden Tesco's Club card, appear to swipe, only to discover the door is already open.

You walk through.

# STAR GAZING

Harold Pinter, notoriously difficult, immediately perked up when I asked him a question relating to a particular point in a little-known television play of his. When talking to celebrities, it is always better, if you can, to ask a question that suggests you have deeper, and much thought about, knowledge of their work than the average sycophant.

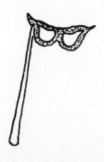

Actors, by the very choice of their profession, are not usually gifted with high-calibre brains. (Interviewing an actor about the content of a film they're in is like asking the printer, rather than the author, about a novel.) A lack of intelligence, in fact, is an advantage, since the dumb actor is more reliant on the author's intentions. Consequently, most actors are particularly flattered if your questions suggest an assumption of prodigious mental powers on their part.

One other rule when talking to celebrities is always talk to them in terms of their success, especially if it is patently obvious they no longer have any.

# It's Only Rock'n'Roll

As with a nightclub, the arrival of gatecrashers is expected at film previews and rock-star parties with greater assurance than the arrival of the guests themselves. Liggers are as inevitable as flies on a turd. In the case of rock-star party (but not the film première), certain girl crashers may be allowed entry for unspecified reasons.

However, your best credential for a film première is your black bow tie (or an LBD).

# Lights, Cameras

One cold evening, I joined the fans behind a barrier
outside a cinema, a scarf covering my tie, my toes
brushing the edge of a grubby red
carpet. A little pulse of electricity
passed through the crowd as the
limo convoy arrived. Stars popped
out, motor winds purred: there was
the bald man from *EastEnders*; wasn't that what's-
her-face from the coffee advert? A flop of dark hair
issuing from a back seat told everyone that Hugh
Grant was here at last. Others were rapidly
following, including a minor celebrity I recognised
but could not name. As all attention was on Hugh, I
ducked under the barrier and stepped just behind
the minor celebrity. Now minus my scarf, I entered
the cinema foyer. All eyes were still on Hugh Grant
and, with the minor celebrity (whose name I still
don't recall) now by my side, I was in.

# People You Might Meet On Your Way

**Michael Winner** You must always talk to Mr Winner about the films he's directed (not the ones he's produced) particularly his self-confessed masterpiece, *Death Wish*.

**Rod Stewart** Although football is a guaranteed subject, what will intrigue him more are his other interests: train-sets and Pre-Raphaelite paintings.

**Jilly Cooper** If you need a brief alibi when crashing a party, Ms Cooper will offer an immediately comforting, gappy smile, not question your presence, and will talk about anything, especially horses.

**John Cleese** Psychologically delicate by his own admission, Mr Cleese can be coaxed into long conversation by a drip-feed of very careful flattery. (Flattery must always be indirect, say, in the form of a question, along the lines of, but in no way as gross as, 'Do you find it difficult dealing with universal fame?')

**Tom Cruise** Mr Cruise is as easy-going as he appears to be in his masterpiece *Cocktail.* You can be sure he won't question you as a ligger and is as safe a bet as Ms Cooper.

**Terry Waite** Perhaps from being incarcerated for so long, Mr Waite is very keen to talk. At a party I crashed at the Dorchester, it was he, astonishingly, who approached me. Mr Waite is a safe bet, being a Christian.

**Ian Hislop** I met Mr Hislop in the lavatory of the Polish Club, during a *Private Eye* party. (Unless it's George Michael, lavatories are good places to meet celebrities as, like death, they tend to make everyone equal.) He is friendly, with a crisp mind but, as with all comedians, it is wise never to try to be funny with him. The rule for comedians is that they must always be treated with extreme seriousness.

**Robbie Williams** In the case of Mr Williams, the opposite is true. Since he thinks he is funnier than he is, it is best to laugh at anything he says.

**Prince Philip** Prince Philip is certainly in the right job: he likes a good party. Perhaps marrying the Queen was, on his part, a very subtle, if extreme, form of gatecrashing.

# Specialisation

Even if, for most people, all parties end the same way with intoxication, fornication or both, every party, to begin with, is unique. Although forward planning is advisable, it is only when you arrive at the Magic Door itself that a realistic plan of action can be formulated. By now you are familiar with the considerable array of techniques available, and should adapt freely. For instance, if you arrive at a party guarded by two guest-listed heavies, you'll immediately recognise the classic theatre or opera entry set-up (*see ENTERING THE TWILIGHT ZONE page 162*), and should respond with the classic theatre-crashing technique.

Nevertheless, there are parties that need individual attention: the crashing method needs to be tailor-made.

One evening, at a concert hall which housed one of the national orchestras, I noticed party activity emanating from a room. Canapés and sandwiches filled round, white-clothed tables: champagne-loaded trays hovered with the agility of UFOs. The guests' invitation cards were in the form of concert tickets. I'd discovered the corporate members' bar.

Most of the arts that are of little interest to people out for a good time are sponsored by numerous corporate bodies. This is partly philanthropy, mainly advertising, and lastly so they can offer employees, as a tax-efficient reward, a night at the opera. One of the benefits is the complimentary corporate bar, allowing the rewarded employees – those out for a good time – to pre-soak their brains in alcohol so as to sustain themselves through the evening's entertainment.

I soon noticed the only people who didn't need to show their tickets were the orchestra players themselves. Having finished their rehearsals, they were encouraged to mingle with and talk to corporate guests, although they seemed more intent, as were the guests, in anaesthetising themselves for the performance.

The orchestra members dress in tails and bow ties. The bow tie is white. A glimpse of the uniform by the official is enough: he nods, smiles and turns back to his daydream.

Disguising myself as an orchestra member, although getting me effortlessly past the official, would lay me open to the orchestra. The coincidence of a corporate guest wearing tails and a white bow tie would, even in their champagne-clouded daze, invite suspicion. The answer lay in that superficial glimpse given to the official.

At the next concert I wore my Armani and a white tie – a long white tie. I also held a thin blue scarf. At the Moment of Maximum Stampede, I followed a couple of orchestra members through the Magic Door, offering a little wave to someone in the room, just as the official looked up. Once in the room, I draped the scarf, as an added precaution, loosely round my neck, half-covering the tie.

I go regularly now, and if the champagne has been particularly effective, occasionally even crash the concert.

On one occasion, as I was sitting at one of the tables reading the complimentary programme, one of the organisers introduced herself.

'Are you one of the orchestra or are you just pretending to be?'

She laughed before I did.

# ENTERING THE TWILIGHT ZONE

Theatre, concert, opera, ballet and exhibition crashing

Whether Bateman's subject taking a fountain pen's worth of ink from a hotel is guilty of theft may be a moot point of law. How much soap, lavatory paper, paper napkins, salt sachets, plastic cutlery can you appropriate from a public place before it becomes a criminal act?

Counsel might say, in the case of lavatory paper, for instance, that you may use as much as would normally be required. However, should you be in an Indian restaurant and suffering a case of sudden and acute diarrhoea (not an unusual occurrence), a roll or two of lavatory paper might be deemed modest for the job in hand. Even so, there are certain boundaries which, once crossed, mean you have taken an unequivocal first step into the magistrate's courtroom.

This is beyond the Twilight Zone. You follow the advice in this chapter at your own risk.

There are books available on how to build a letter bomb, how to pick a three-tumbler mortice-lock, break into a car, to extract yourself from a pair of police handcuffs.

*Expert At The Card-Table,* however, is a classic text in the art of card manipulation. Most of it is, in fact, a comprehensive series of lessons on how to cheat. Offered as information to the honest card player for the purpose of spotting a

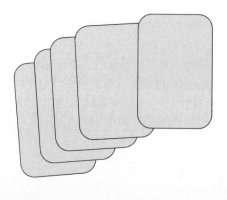

sharp, the painful attention to detail – exact descriptions and illustrations on finger-positions, step-by-step instructions – might seem excessive, almost tempting the honest card player to have a go him- or herself.

In my own case, I offer the following information, of course, solely as a warning to the security of the listed public places, like a journalist planting a bomb in a plane.

# A Night At The Opera

If a dentist sees a person's face as all teeth, a professional thief sees the world as a place of open doors. The thief doesn't have that covetous nausea you might feel on seeing a particular piece of Tiffany jewelry, or an Yves St Laurent suit, or a Cartier watch in a shop window. The thief doesn't see a window, but an open display inviting tactile contemplation or acquisition: a free dip.

It's a world peculiarly bereft of security: valuable objects can be made to float way at any time.

For the top-flight crasher, the doors are open too. In exactly the same way you might pass a shop and fancy a browse, the crasher will, with time on their hands, pass the Royal Academy, or the Haymarket Theatre, and decide on a quick look round the Monet exhibition or to watch the first act of a West End thriller. They might, after leaving a bar, decide to catch the opening of an opera, just as you might decide, while shopping, to try a taste of wine in a supermarket promotion.

# THEATRE, CONCERTS, OPERA BALLET, THEATRE – ON THE HOUSE

# How To Do It

In certain films, the sex scenes are so well simulated that they're indistinguishable from the real thing. (Sometimes you wonder why they bother to simulate it. Sometimes you wonder if they do bother.)

In the same way, a conjuror simulates familiar actions so closely that, even though the true action is doing something else, your eye accepts it as unsuspicious. There's no more elegant example than that of dealing from the bottom of a pack of cards. If skillfully executed, dealing from the bottom, by an artful tilt of the pack, exactly simulates a top deal.

Crashing theatres uses the same device of illusion through simulation.

Crashing theatres is like faking sex.

Sometimes I think the Theatre Crash is so aesthetically pleasing that any theatre proprietor possessed of the least artistic sensibility spotting you executing it would be obliged to concede you a seat out of sheer awe.

You may have noticed I've excluded cinemas from my list. This is due to the simple fact that whereas theatre-, opera- and concertgoers are trusted, cinema audiences are not. The security measures reflect this. This might seem curious, as the former is usually more expensive than the latter.

However, there may be some basis of truth in the assumption. In theatre, opera and concert bars, pre-paid interval drinks are left on the bar shelves to be picked up. Although intervals in cinemas are now rare, you have the distinct feeling that, if the same service were available, the drinks would have long since disappeared before the rightful customers had seen them or even left their seats.

Trust, the godsend of confidence tricksters, thieves and liggers, makes theatre, opera and concerts a socialist ideal, available to all.

# The Set-Up

The method is partly dependent on the assumption of the Magic Door being guarded by two ticket collectors. From this you'd expect the perpetration to be doubly daunting, as do the proprietors, but in fact it makes it possible. One reason two ticket collectors are employed is because of the sudden rush of audience at the curtain call, when they debouch from the adjacent bars. This cascade of bodies is, of course, advantageous to you: it's the Moment Of Maximum Stampede.

# The Sting

 As the audience engulfs the doorway, the two ticket collectors become fully employed, tearing not just individual tickets, but clumps of group bookings. You approach holding your own ticket (it is barely visible, since, in fact, you're not holding anything). You go to the nearest collector as he or she is particularly busy. Just before reaching them, with your hand semi-proffered, you turn: now your hand is semi-proffered to the second collector. Just before you reach him or her, your hand is already lowering, and now you find yourself already in the auditorium.

You have achieved what the instructions with magic tricks call The Effect: the first collector believes, because they were busy, you turned to the second collector. With your back now obscuring any subsequent transaction from him or her, your hand is now lowering itself to the second collector, who assumes you've just handed your ticket to the first collector.

Both collectors believe the other took your ticket.

## Group Sex

Most West End theatre reflects the tastes of the tourist market, in that the plays put on are, like coffee, instant, universally popular and nutritionally redundant. If theatre management ever venture to classics, they require a star. *Hamlet* would need Arnold Schwarzenegger. However, the tourists provide the crasher with another means of entry.

## EXITS AND ENTRANCES

*One of the fortunate facts of theatres, opera houses and concert halls, is that there are many levels and entrances to the auditorium. Every entrance is a possibility, the number of entrances multiplying, by that amount, your chances of entry. If one is impossible, simply try the next.*

There is no more pleasurable sight for the theatre crasher than the arrival of an animated group-booked party. Like a gaggle of geese, it creates diversion and a moment of intense activity for the ticket collectors. The gaggle tends to pass the collectors even as they are counting the clump of tickets, leaving it too late for them to count the individuals in the group.

Crashing the theatre is, of course, a simple matter of joining them. Japanese group bookings are common, but even these are not exempt, for the English theatre-crasher can pose as one of the guides. Of course, if you are a Japanese crasher, you have a distinct advantage.

# The Best In The House

A helpful service supplied by the box-office is to inform the theatre crasher which seats are available, and which are the best. A fortuitous bonus is that the seats most available are usually the most expensive, since they're the least likely to be sold.

On one occasion, when I failed to do this, I gradually realised the stalls, where I'd found myself, were completely booked. Once the seats were all filled, the ticket collector approached.

'The performance is about to begin, sir.'

'Yes, I think I should've been in the circle. I'm supposed to be joining my wife but I can't see her.'

'Can I see your ticket, sir?'

'I think I've dropped it. But you took the other half. Is it alright if I just sit on the steps?'

'Can't do that sir. Fire risk. But there is a spare seat in the balcony – if we hurry.'

As it happens, I left after ten minutes. It must've been *The Mousetrap*.

# No Pressure

When in the auditorium you must wait for everyone else to be seated. If an official asks if they can help, you merely say you're waiting for your partner.

As I suggested above, about 90 per cent of current West End drama has the intellectual content of a ham omelette, but this is not reflected in the price. Theatre, opera and concerts are notoriously expensive.

In this respect, the crasher has, apart from not paying anything, a considerable advantage over the rest of the audience: he or she can leave at any time, within five minutes of the curtain rising. The remainder of the audience, even if they have to sit through another three hours of uninhibited stupidity, are clamped to their seats by their own tiny-hearted meanness.

In the same way that part of a psychiatrist's treatment is dependent on the expense to the patient, theatregoers, because they've paid so much, can even convince themselves that what they're watching is good.

One of the pleasures for the crasher, in fact, is to notice the stunned faces of their neighbours as you leave after ten minutes. They probably assume you're a critic – or the author.

The hurried pre-theatre supper – knocking back a lump of poached salmon and a bottle of Chablis with ten minutes until curtain call – can be a stressful arrangement. Here, the theatre crasher has another advantage. The crasher doesn't need to see the whole play or concert in the same evening. After watching the first act, the evening can be concluded with an early, though lengthy, dinner.

The following night, or four or five weeks later, you can begin with a protracted supper, followed by the second act (which, of course, doesn't require a ticket check). I particularly enjoy this arrangement since it allows me to contemplate the first act at my leisure and, more importantly, gives me time to consider whether it's even worth going back.

# Summer In The City

One June evening – one of those summer nights when people loiter in streets for nothing, apparently, other than the pleasure of existing, experiencing the energy from other people, sunlit windows, and the city's own excited heart – I remember crashing an early party at the National Portrait Gallery.

After enjoying some smoked salmon decorated with caviar and a Sauvignon Blanc, I wandered out and, passing a theatre, crashed the first act of what, amazingly, was a watchable play. It was still light and warm as I then walked up the Strand to my favourite haunt, The Savoy, where I was just in time for a generous corporate dinner and cabaret.

The evening was so enjoyable I caught a bus back – and paid the fare.

# The Theatre's Friend

There is a good argument, though not legally satisfying, for the crasher being a benefit to any theatre. Both actors and proprietors enjoy the sight of 'bums on seats'; the actors feel wanted, the proprietors feel rich.

The crasher, of course, can only ever sit on an unsold seat. Provided he or she had no intention of buying a ticket, the theatre loses nothing by being crashed: it only gains by looking more populated.

I discovered, incidentally, that one well-known West End theatre has an entrance into the auditorium perpetually unstaffed. I wonder if this is deliberate, the proprietors having decided that the crasher is an asset and should be cultivated.

# How Far Can You Go?

Later in this book, I will comment on the danger of
moral disintegration inherent in prolonged crashing
– analogous to the mental decay of drug addicts –
but it's worth mentioning here an early warning
sign: THE INTERVAL DRINKS TEST.

The crasher becomes addicted to the freebee. Reaching a certain stage in your theatre-crashing career, you'll become increasingly aware of the line of pre-bought drinks adorning the bar shelves at the intervals. Your natural ability to refrain from appropriating these becomes gradually harder to sustain, not so much because you're desperate for a drink, but simply because this completely outrageous display of trust affronts your sensibility. Like an open safe, it's too much.

You anticipate, as you sit in your aisle seat, the pre-interval act is about to end. As the curtain falls, you are already ahead of everyone in the bar rush. You must now wait for the bar staff to become occupied. Then, lifting the receipt from under a glass, you inspect it, then take two drinks. This can be done quite calmly, since the least hurried members of the audience going to the bar will be the ones who have pre-ordered their drinks.

Once you have the glasses, though, immediately ascend or descend stairs to the furthest theatre bar from your own. Here, you place one drink a little away from you on a shelf (anyone hunting you will be looking for someone with two glasses). Consume at your leisure.

As you sip your drink, listening to conversation tortuously bent on constructive comments about the play – 'the lighting is excellent.' 'Oh, yes, there's no problem about being able to see it' – you'll have time to absorb the extent of this moral gearshift, and to contemplate your true descent into the hardcore gatecrasher's mentality.

# THE DRINKS ARE ON THEM

This leads me naturally to the subject of bar-crashing. You may be pleased, even relieved to know that bar-crashing, like cardsharping, is completely legal, if equally unscrupulous.

As someone who keeps to rules – those of my own making, that is, not anyone else's – I rigorously keep to the one of never drinking alone. The extent I will go to achieve this would be understood if you witnessed some of the company I've had to keep. It has even brought into question the very definition of 'company'.

At the moment I define company as a mammal which knows a minimum of four words of English. By the rules of my own game, if I haven't any company, I must crash a party or visit a bar.

Although parsimony is a motivation for all gatecrashing, it is also a point of honour among crashers to pay as little as possible for anything.

Finding myself paying for a glass of wine in a bar for what would normally buy a bottle in a supermarket, my natural crasher instincts were aroused. I became steadily more resentful, until I began to view it as an insidious form of theft.

It was shortly after visiting a bar in Covent Garden, then walking a few yards to Tesco Metro directly opposite and seeing the same bottle for a third of the price, that I developed the bar-crashing techniques outlined here.

# Happy Hour Every Hour

If I'm meeting a friend, I usually contrive to arrange it at Brown's in Covent Garden, an All Bar One, or any other bar with which I am familiar.

When the friend arrives, they find on the table a bottle of expensive wine and two glasses, sometimes a gin and tonic if they enjoy one to begin with. Seeing my generosity, they are only too pleased to buy the next drinks.

Neither the bar staff nor my friend are aware that all the drinks supplied by me have, in fact, been supplied by Tesco Metro just up the street.

For the economically minded of you, this might seem almost as impressive – and almost as useful – as turning water into wine. (Of Jesus's miracles, this one impressed me more than the Resurrection itself.) The basic principle is, of course, when visiting a bar you always bring your own.

Since explanations should be simple and direct, I'll begin with the simplest drink – the humble (though large) glass of red wine.

Although supermarkets supply small bottles of wine, I prefer to decant standard-sized bottles into plastic mineral water bottles, which are, of course, also wine-tight. I have a selection of water bottles, depending on the evening's arrangements, but 250-cc water bottles are portable, discreet – and three will carry a full bottle of wine.

The bar must be relatively busy. You can ask for a glass at the bar (to join friends who have bought a bottle). Alternatively, like the wine, you can bring your own, but make sure it matches the bar's.

A third method is to pick up a used glass and wash it in the lavatory. It will probably then be cleaner than when offered to the original customer.

Then, with the glass held so that it cannot be seen to be empty, you stroll to the lavatory, find a cubicle, and fill (with wine, I mean). You can keep another, full mineral bottle in a jacket inner breast pocket, or your handbag: in an isolated alcove, you can replenish the glass at any time *in situ*, without need of lavatorial assistance.

The principle is the same for spirits. These drinks can be pre-mixed, as can cocktails. Ice and lemon are available at the bar on request.

## TRADE HINT 1

*If you are opening cans of lager or tonic water in the lavatory cubicle, you'll need to adopt Jack Nicholson's method in* Chinatown *(synchronising a sneeze with ripping out a page from the local voting register). Flushing the loo is the best course, or wait for someone to use the hand-drier or be sick.*

# TRADE HINT 2

*Wines and beers can be kept cool by keeping in zip-up wine coolers, those resembling a diving suit without arms. Alternatively, a freezer wrapper, resembling a chrome lifejacket, used to chill a bottle rapidly, can effectively maintain low temperatures.*

# Saving For Later

The mineral bottle technique can, for the severely economically minded, easily be reversed – instead of dispensing alcohol, it can be used for storing.

If you are following my guidelines on drink consumption, you may lament the fine wines denied to you at a party after your limit has been reached. As a means of forestalling temptation, the wine can be stored for the following day instead.

Simply take two glasses and retire to your cubicle, and here, over the lavatory bowl, pour into the mineral bottle. Even champagne can be stored successfully, as long as your bottle is filled level with the top and immediately sealed.

Depending on the quantity of your mineral bottle arsenal, you can return to the lavatory as many times as you like. No-one will notice as, becoming increasingly intoxicated, they will be in need of frequent visits themselves.

# LAVATORY LARKS

I once visited a public lavatory in Clapham, and was surprised to find it full. As I peed, I slowly became aware, because of the sound of my solo trickle, that no one else was peeing. I then heard from a cubicle two men in whispered discussion. It wasn't so much their conversation which disturbed me, but the sporadic, quizzical yelps of their dog. I noticed on a later visit to Clapham, the lavatory had been boarded up.

Because of such associations with public lavatories, most people using them are over-anxious to keep themselves to themselves. (In fact, from what I've seen and heard in lavatories, my own activities could almost be viewed as virtuous.) This makes the lavatory as equally conducive to the gatecrasher as to the Ecstasy consumer. From changing into your black tie, storing or dispensing drinks, or wrapping party food in napkins, this is where you can momentarily relax, assured of privacy and security.

Treat the lavatory like home.

# A Friend In Need

It's difficult to find a friend who is totally honest, but equally difficult to find one totally uncorrupted by moral or human values. However, if like-minded people can be brought together (perhaps this book may inspire the formation of little societies, like a rambling or poetry club), bar and restaurant crashing can be notably enhanced.

Not only does it mean you needn't hide your deception among your friends, and that your bottle carrying capacity is increased, but also that extra cover – as useful as a wood on a battlefield – is afforded by your friends' physical presence. With a couple of friends, bottles can be switched and glasses filled with ease.

The very act of deception can give a sense of adventure a night at the pub would otherwise lack. The planning, the choosing of the wines or cocktails and venues has an excitement of its own. There is also the added satisfaction that after your evening's entertainment, your wallet, if you bothered bringing it, will remain in its virginal state.

Instead of looking for new friends, you might like to approach your present ones. Take care, however. On learning of your proposals, they might then want to reassess their friendship.

# A Lot Of Bottle

The best that even a waiter will say about a house wine is that it is 'passable'.

Yet almost inevitably, after looking down the wine list, and seeing the most basic Chilean Merlot at £20.00 (*Special Offer at Tesco's: £3.29*), you hear yourself saying, 'Well, should we try the house wine? I'm sure it's good here.'

Now when I look at the wine list, in my mind's eye, the prices have been crossed through, rather like this:

# DRASTIC REDUCTIONS!!!

**Pouilly Fumé, was £40.00 – NOW £8.00!**

**Veuve Cliquot Brut, was £75.00 – NOW £40.00!**

**House Wines, were £12.00 – OUR PRICE, an ASTOUNDING £3.00!**

*UNBELIEVABLE PRICES! BUY NOW!'*

The principle is the same as with the glass, but obviously you can't introduce a bottle to the bar or restaurant that they don't stock.

As with any military strategy, before attacking you'll need to reconnoitre the terrain, either to find a wine they have that you can buy in a shop, or, a safer gambit, to borrow one of their empties.

The empty bottle is then washed, and, when you are ready for your outing, your own bottle is decanted into it. Put a stopper on the bottle, the bottle in your bag.

In the bar, withdraw the bottle discreetly, and the glass if you have one. Pour a little into the glass, and you're ready to meet your friend.

As many prepared bottles as you like can be stored in your bag (but wrap each in cloth to avoid the drinks' trolley jingle).

Although it's irrelevant, apart from the colour, that the wine should match the name on the bottle, if your friend for the evening is not party to your deception, it is wise to match it as much as possible.

Having said that, given the state of most people's palates, they probably wouldn't even notice a discrepancy in colour.

## TRUE COLOURS

It is advisable to fill the
bottle with the same colour
of wine as the original:
putting a Claret into a
Chardonnay bottle might
alert the more
knowledgeable of wine
waiters.

To bring your own bottle to a restaurant, it is essential that the restaurant has a separate – and busy – bar area. The procedure is exactly the same, except, once you've poured your glass, you proceed to the restaurant, carrying both bottle and glass to the table.

If your friend is in the know, you can both take bottles in, claiming that you'd both bought them, not realising the other had arrived – or simply admit that you are both alcoholics and like a bottle each.

# BUY ONE, GET TEN FREE – THE HOTEL

When staying at a hotel, I like to arrive between 4.00 and 5.00 p.m. Like a hospital ward, it is the time when a soporific cloud seeps down the corridors, a lull in the afternoon, affecting staff and guests alike. The Moment Of Inattention is indefinitely sustained.

Guests nod deep in armchairs, waiting for tea, waiters eat late lunches, staff change over for the late shift, there's a tinkle from the kitchen as a solitary cook stirs his coffee.

This is the time to inspect the premises – reception rooms (party or dinner preparations will be evident), restaurant table layout, but most importantly, the unstaffed bar.

Stretching over the bar, I take a wine glass, assured then of an evening of good Chablis Grand Cru. The only other consideration, which you should already have noted, is that the dining room tables have tablecloths.

Members of the Mafia and free-lance hitmen, when eating at restaurants, like to sit with their backs to a wall and facing the entrance. When you enter the hotel restaurant you should insist on the same (ideally, a corner table), except, rather than the entrance, a view of the waiter's kitchen exit.

This is a good position for your breakfast too, if you wish to stock up at the buffet on cold meats, boiled eggs, cheeses, yoghurts, fruit, bread, butter sachets and individual mini-jam pots for your packed or picnic lunch.

The method of acquisition is simple. Throughout breakfast, at appropriate moments, you collect the food you'll need on a plate, together with some paper napkins, then spread the open napkins on your lap. During Moments Of Inattention – of both waiters and guests – place cold meats and cheeses on the napkins, fold and wrap and deposit in your shoulder bag or briefcase.

To facilitate this, I usually bring work with me to the table – papers, books, pens – making dips into my bag seem more credible. If a particularly lavish buffet has been laid on, it seems to me to be almost criminal not to express gratitude for the hotel's generosity. So try and take even more than you need for your packed lunch.

On occasions, I've hardly been able to lift my shoulder bag by the end of breakfast. I've enjoyed several days of hotel cuisine after only a one-night visit.

You now enter the restaurant with your first glass of Chablis, poured out either in your room, or a downstairs lavatory near the bar. The remainder of the Chablis lies in water bottles in your shoulder bag. If you're wearing a jacket, one of the bottles may be lodged in your inside breast pocket.

Now you'll appreciate the tablecloth. Like a curtain, or the lap-draped raincoat of a pervert, any number of negotiations can take place beneath the level of the table top. A whole model army could be set up down there, a chess game, a portable TV set.

Place the linen napkin on your lap, and the first water bottle under it between your legs. At this point, if you're male, the pervert's raincoat analogy will seem even more apt.

As your meal progresses, you drink, making sure the glass remains three-quarters full. Throughout the dinner you'll need to refill the glass so that it appears to remain undrunk. This is easily accomplished during Moments Of Inattention (or, given most hotel restaurants, moments – hours – of sheer absence), by lowering the glass to your lap, and filling it with the water bottle.

If you're staying for more than one night, it's worth retiring to the bar with your glass, so you can retain it for the rest of your stay.

The waiters, although impressed by your abstemiousness of only one glass of wine, may be surprised by the effect it's had on your speech and your short walk from the restaurant.

Occasionally, the bar is locked or too closely guarded to take a glass. The safest option is to buy your first glass, and refill with your own. The drawback of this is that you'll need to mix your own wine with theirs. Malcolm Gluck, the author of *Superplonk*, maintains this might be an advantage. At a party of his I crashed, he told me how he often mixes wines to make a more interesting taste. Here is opportunity to experiment.

# THE LONELINESS OF THE LONG-DISTANCE GATECRASHER

I always wake up at 5.30 a.m. to begin work. This morning, Big Ben's chime was as clear and determined as the blue of the sky, the first sky of summer. That blackbird was busier than usual, noisier, as if competing with the clock, or even the morning. As usual, the title of Mailer's book *What Are We Doing In Vietnam?* struck me again. I had been at two parties and a dinner last night and that title, changed to *What Are We Doing At This Party?*, came to mind each time I passed through the Magic Door. Every morning now, about a minute after I open my eyes, the question returns: sometimes it broadens to 'What Are We Doing Alone In This Flat?', occasionally as far as 'What Are We Doing On This Planet?'

I got up, made the bed, taking care over the hospital corners. I exercised, washed, threw away the menu of The Royal Institute of Psychiatrist's Annual Dinner, left on the breakfast table last night, and then made my porridge. As I ate, I thought of the letter in the *Evening Standard*.

Two years ago the paper interviewed me about gatecrashing, provoking a woman to write in, asking, 'Hasn't Nicholas Allan got anything better to do in his evenings?' I thought lengthily, even broodingly, about this, and in the end came up with the answer: no.

I've noticed, recently, how I relish crashing a concert more than the prospect of hearing it: I think about leaving a play as soon as the curtain rises. I read a novel for the prose style, not for the characters in it, nor for feelings a novel is supposed to engender.

It's begun to make me question how far gatecrashing has affected any deeper yearnings I might have had to become a complete and integrated person.

Gatecrashing has taken me on a long-haul journey in a certain direction. Whether I chose to pursue gatecrashing because I was morally ambivalent to begin with, or whether crashing has brought it about, is difficult to tell, but I do know that it has definitely exacerbated the disease. Over three years, I've now reached a point, where, if even remotely challenged at a party, I'm genuinely upset and put out, as if I have a right to trespass, lie and steal. I find it difficult to truly see what I'm doing wrong, why they should object.

As I drink tea, LBC news tells me three children with a gun threatened other kids to hand over their ice-creams. The natural indignation and worry over moral standards by a commentator seemed to me alien, even suspect. I couldn't believe that someone could be genuinely appalled or surprised by it. Like the kids in *Lord Of The Flies*, the children with the gun were behaving quite naturally. They wanted something and they happened to have the means – excessive for the job, admittedly – to acquire it.

The constant deception of gatecrashing – the daily habit of lying – leads you into a private world, probably like that of a successful hitman. Honesty, and – as Saul Bellow puts it – 'disinterested charity' in other people is one of the few things that move me, even if I'm simultaneously bemused.

I lost my belief in Santa when about five, in God at 13, and began to seriously question moral belief in my twenties. These are all beliefs that we've been taught. More insidiously, the ability to feel has been taught to us too. Nietzsche pointed out that science is as dependent on belief as religion – everything is an invention. Feelings for other people, even being in love, are concepts we've been brought up to accept, learning them like sums and grammar. It's no coincidence that the biographies of psychopaths often reveal childhoods lacking in parental (or any other) guidance.

Edmund White's roman-à-clef, *The Farewell Symphony*, tells of a great poet who shows his friends a new piece of work. They think it's brilliant, but tentatively suggest it's a little cold. 'Oh!' says the poet, 'I forgot to put the feeling in!' He rushes upstairs, is gone for an hour, then returns with the poem. His friends read it and are moved to tears.

Sounds of innocence – the chirrup of thrushes squabbling in the treetop level with my kitchen window, its leaves baubles of fluorescent green, lit by a low sun – made me wonder if it's possible to re-learn what you think you've lost. Once a belief has gone can you teach yourself to believe in it again? Could I seriously learn to re-believe in Santa, or the Tooth Fairy, or my childhood friend, Mr Eebee Geebees, who lived under the oven?

In his notebooks, Camus wrote 'Seek excess in moderation' (which didn't stop him killing himself by driving excessively fast). All addiction is excess and leads inescapably to some form of corruption. Gatecrashing is an addiction. The need, like that of a drug addict, finally overrides any consideration for others. Deceit becomes, not only natural, but preferable.

So, increasingly I wake up now and decide to have a go at being more human again, as an experiment, something different, a bit of a laugh. One habit can be turned into another. Just as habitual lying every evening permeates my daily conversation too, I can make a habit of being truthful instead. However, the question the letter writer in the *Standard* put still remains unanswered. I wonder how she spends her evenings: reading the *Evening Standard* and writing letters?

A television phobic, due to a massive parental overdose when a child, I sit in a silent flat. I try to avoid music, books and films if possible as they interfere with writing. Perhaps, like Kafka, I should do woodwork classes.

I could spend more time on my German course, begin to collect Ordnance Survey Maps, or read the *Evening Standard* and write letters. As part of my self-therapy, I could volunteer as a night porter at St Thomas' Hospital down the road.

Alternatively, I could re-learn that most mysterious and elusive of arts – falling into and sustaining love. I could get married, have children. I could become...involved.

Does every criminal harbour a little part of themselves – of which they may be unaware – that yearns to be caught? Even if only in prison, at last you would no longer need to maintain a pretence, harbour a secret. You could be what you are, and learn to be better.

Richard Klein wrote *Cigarettes are Sublime*, an elegant and thoughtful book about smoking, and claimed that it was only by writing the book that he finally managed to give up smoking himself. I suggested at the beginning of this book that there was a last reason for writing it: the simple reason of wanting to quit. I want to go legitimate, to make a fresh start in life: I want to be a decent, kind-hearted, altruistic person – someone you'd like to invite to your party.

I might succeed – or be forced to by the exposure from this book. If you take up the methods I've suggested and go to parties too, you might learn if I've succeeded or not.

If I haven't, I'll be seeing you there.